D1594364

SEMI-CIVILIZED

Frontispiece. A group of Samal Moros in the Moro Village at the Louisiana
Purchase Exposition

SEMI-CIVILIZED

The Moro Village at the Louisiana Purchase Exposition

MICHAEL C. HAWKINS

NORTHERN ILLINOIS UNIVERSITY PRESS
AN IMPRINT OF
CORNELL UNIVERSITY PRESS
ITHACA AND LONDON

A volume in the NIU Southeast Asian Series

Edited by Kenton Clymer

For a list of books in the series visit our website
at cornellpress.cornell.edu.

First published 2020 by Cornell University Press

Library of Congress Cataloging-in-Publication Data

Names: Hawkins, Michael (Michael C.), author.
Title: Semi-civilized : the Moro village at the Louisiana Purchase
    Exposition/Michael C. Hawkins.
Description: Ithaca, New York : Northern Illinois University Press, an
    imprint of Cornell University Press, 2020. | Series: NIU Southeast Asian
    series | Includes bibliographical references and index.
Identifiers: LCCN 2019026549 (print) | LCCN 2019026550 (ebook) |
    ISBN 9781501748219 (hardcover) | ISBN 9781501748226 (epub) |
    ISBN 9781501748233 (pdf)
Subjects: LCSH: Louisiana Purchase Exposition (1904 : Saint Louis, Mo.) |
    Muslims—Philippines—Exhibitions—History—20th century. |
    Ethnology—Philippines—Exhibitions—History—20th century. | Human
    zoos—Missouri—Saint Louis—History—20th century. | Imperialism in
    popular culture—Missouri—Saint Louis—History—20th century.
Classification: LCC DS666.M8 H395 2020 (print) | LCC DS666.M8
    (ebook) | DDC 305.6/970977866074—dc23
LC record available at https://lccn.loc.gov/2019026549
LC ebook record available at https://lccn.loc.gov/2019026550

Contents

PREFACE

The Louisiana Purchase Exposition of 1904 was by far the largest world's fair ever organized. Occupying 1,272 acres on St. Louis's west side, on what is now Forest Park and the campus of Washington University, the exposition took in nearly twenty million visitors over eight months. The fifteen-million-dollar project drew participation from forty-three American states and more than sixty countries. The German immigrant George Kessler's elaborate design consisted of fifteen hundred structures, which included twelve major exhibit buildings and a hotel known as the "Inside Inn" with two thousand rooms and a capacity of forty-five hundred people.[1] More than seventy-five miles of internal roads and walking paths laced the fairgrounds. An additional fifteen miles of double-track railways circled the event with seventeen different stops. These amenities were designed to "assure the highest degree of convenience, ease, and comfort for visitors who [came] to inspect the wonders contained within its enclosure."[2] Electric lights, in their "most striking and most effective form," lined the avenues "so liberally" that the "Exposition grounds and buildings [blazed] with light at night" so as to "rival the attractions of daylight."[3] Led by the "Apotheosis of St. Louis," fair organizers commissioned more than one thousand sculptures at a cost of five hundred thousand dollars. The fair's main thoroughfare, known simply as "The Pike," boasted over fifty world-class attractions from every part of the globe. Never had an event been so publicized. In a single month preceding the opening of the exposition 1,848,960 lines of newsprint across the country, excluding St. Louis, heralded and described every aspect of the impending event. This amounted to an average of 431,424 words a day.[4] Despite the exposition's global and even "universal" scope, the fair was ultimately an unabashed celebration of American modernity. The centenary of the Louisiana Purchase provided a broadly recognizable historical marker to gauge the United States' rapid ascent to global and industrial prominence. Exposition president David R. Francis proclaimed the exposition

> [an] obligation on the part of the people of the Louisiana Purchase Territory to give expression of their gratitude for the innumerable blessings that have flowed from a century of membership in the American Union, to manifest their appreciation of the manifold benefits of living in a land, the climate and soil and resources of which are unsurpassed, and of having their lots cast in an age when liberty and enlightenment are established on foundations broad and deep, and are the heritage of all who worthily strive.

For Francis the peoples of the Louisiana Purchase Territory personified the American "impulse to excel," which "operates in the United States with an aggressive force seldom exhibited in other countries." The St. Louis Fair thus offered an unprecedented opportunity for millions of visitors from around the world to learn from and pay homage to America's achievements. "The far-reaching effect of such a vast display of man's best works on the intelligent and emulous minds of fifty or sixty millions of students, is beyond computation," marveled Francis. "Man's competitive instinct, the spontaneous lever that arouses human activity and exalts human effort, directing it to higher standards of excellence, will surely work with a high potential current here."[5]

Such sentiments had added significance in 1904. Six years prior to the exposition, the United States had suddenly acquired a vast string of colonial possessions spanning thousands of miles across the Pacific and the Caribbean. Like the Louisiana Purchase Territory a century before,

US colonies provided a new frontier with unprecedented opportunities to share and benefit from Americans' "impulse to excel." Nowhere was this more important than in the Philippines. By 1904 the United States had successfully subdued the Philippine insurgency and begun to implement various governmental and cultural institutions. The United States' policy of "benevolent assimilation" was in full bloom.[6] Hence, from the very initial planning phases, fair organizers determined to make the Philippine exhibit a centerpiece of the exposition's message.

The resulting "Philippine Village" consisted of ninety-two total structures spread over forty-seven acres on the southwest side of the fairgrounds. The amalgam of native dwellings, restaurants, exhibit buildings, and service houses for the public cost an astounding $613,418.[7] A Philippine Exposition Board oversaw the collection of seventy thousand exhibits organized into three hundred classes and one hundred groups.[8] By far, however, the most critical aspect of the Philippine Village was its eleven hundred "live exhibits" who were brought in to demonstrate the islands' "wide variety of physical and cultured types."[9] These Filipinos comprised half of all live exhibits at the fair; a massive assemblage of colonial subjects meant to illustrate profound lessons regarding "the life and civilization of a whole people."[10] In this way, the Philippine display was intended to provide a living analogy of human evolution on a grand scale. Fair patrons could theoretically behold the aggregate of humankind's evolutionary journey from savage primitivism to modern civilization, with all of the inherent self-reflexive ponderings that this might provoke.

At the center of this book is a curious subsection of the Philippine exhibit known as the Moro Village—a display comprised of Philippine Muslims from the southern islands of Mindanao and Sulu. My interest was essentially born out of an anonymous 1904 editorial in the *Mindanao Herald*, which offered blunt criticism of the Moro Exhibit after the Louisiana Purchase Exposition. I included this editorial in my first book as a segue into discussions of subsequent expositional efforts in the Philippines. At the time I did not bother to question the sentiments expressed in the *Herald* piece, as it seemed to largely agree with existing literature on the subject. However, in 2015, I published an article examining the 1899 Greater America Exposition in Omaha, Nebraska.[11] This was my first serious foray into deep research on colonial exposition. I quickly discovered that the subject matter offered an unexpectedly profound opportunity for critical insight into imperial discourse and ideology at large. It appeared as a small but remarkably promising entry point to draw larger conclusions about the nature of American empire in the Philippines in unique circumstances.

My mind immediately gravitated back to the editorial in the *Mindanao Herald*. I subsequently began to unravel a surprisingly abundant collection of primary source materials dealing, to greater and lesser degrees, with the Moro experience at the St. Louis World's Fair. My original intent was to compose a substantial article on the Moro Village and then perhaps pursue a larger book project concerning the Philippine exhibit more broadly. I managed to carve out an article but immediately regarded it with the deepest dissatisfaction. So much was left out; so much left unsaid. I consequently set the piece aside and began working on the remaining material. Another article resulted. However, it made much better sense when connected with the first. And there was still material left over. I was frustrated. I set the work aside for several months to focus on teaching and administrative duties. Nevertheless, the project was continually spurred on by presentations at a meeting of the American Academy of Religion and symposiums at the Center for Philippine Studies at the University of Hawaii and the Kripke Center at Creighton University. At last, little by little, I had what appeared to be a book manuscript. The result was a slender, but highly focused, study of the Moro experience at the Louisiana Purchase Exposition. Given its brevity and intensely circumscribed chronology, I have been tempted at times to break the manuscript into four or five articles of typical length. However, I firmly believe that the story needs to be told as a connected whole, despite its narrow scope. The Moros' designation as "semi-civilized" conveys a consistent and critical message throughout the course of their experiences at the fair. It is a message that needs to be presented as a methodological and analytical whole. Hence, I offer the present volume.

Readers will undoubtedly notice a theoretical alliance with the general methods and ideas of "new imperial history" and "subaltern studies." This is an attempt to examine the experiences of a people who were mostly hidden in the sources. Unfortunately, much of Moro history is necessarily and generally related through the prism of American history and overwhelmingly with American sources. This fact forces scholars to deploy innovative methodologies so as to integrate and highlight subaltern historical actors, while carefully allowing them the agency and fallibility extended to those with greater power. It also requires historians to frequently record and analyze the reactions and policies of the colonizers as a conduit to understanding the colonized. This is certainly the case with this book. It is, therefore, the sincere hope of this author that the historical Moros will shine through the haze of decidedly Ameri-centric contexts, circumstances, and sources. However, as with most historical episodes, the Moro experience at the Louisiana Purchase Exposition is a deeply entangled and mutually constitutive story of twentieth-century empire, in which both colonizer and colonized are defined and problematized by their collaborations, antagonisms, and continuously negotiated identities relative to the other.

Acknowledgments

Like any work of substance, this book is the outgrowth of a wealth of influences. Although I cannot adequately acknowledge the myriad of contributions that made this project possible, I will attempt to address a few here. I would first like to thank the College of Arts and Science at Creighton University for providing a generous research grant in the summer of 2014. This award provided the initial means for me to conduct research in the Philippines and thus, in a very real way, gave birth to the project. I would also like to thank the diligent and impeccably professional archivists, librarians, and student workers who guided my often misguided efforts to acquire information. To the attentive and gracious professionals at the Philippine National Library, the passionate and accommodating staff at the various Missouri historical societies, and of course the miracle workers at Interlibrary Loan in Creighton University's Reinert-Alumni Memorial Library, I offer my deepest thanks.

As the chapters began to take shape, I relied on the invaluable insights of numerous colleagues and fellow scholars who helped me polish, refine, and sometimes reconsider my ideas and arguments. In particular, I would like to thank John Calvert, for an early reading of my introduction and theoretical approach, as well as Tracy Leavelle, for our numerous conversations and his multiple invitations to present my work to scholars outside my particular field. The book largely took its shape during this early period. I am also grateful to the commentators, fellow panelists, and audience members who probed the validity and soundness of my scholarship at conferences and seminars and during casual conversations in hotel lobbies and corner cafes. Each criticism and each comment contributed to the final composition of this book. I want to thank my students Brian Boerner and Calvin Fairbourn, who took the time to read portions of the manuscript during independent study courses and offered discerning insights on the book's accessibility and applicability. Finally, I want to extend special appreciation to Timothy Marr and Paul Rodell. Their thorough, thoughtful, and profoundly insightful critique of a later draft was essential to the book's publication. Their professionalism, knowledge, and uncanny eye for detail continually provide a model of true scholarship.

Most of all, I owe a debt of immeasurable gratitude to my dear family. My wife, Eve, and our children, Isaac and Mika, stand as a constant source of support and love. The vicissitudes and inevitable setbacks of research, writing, and publication all fall into their proper context when exposed to the light of family togetherness. If studying history has taught me anything, it is that people are all that matter, and there is no group of people I would rather spend forever with. This book, much like anything else I may accomplish, was a collective effort.

SEMI-CIVILIZED

INTRODUCTION

The Complicated and Collaborative Art
of Colonial Display

As early as 1902 American officials in the Philippines began collecting and organizing exhibits for the Louisiana Purchase Exposition, also known as the 1904 World's Fair, in St. Louis, Missouri. In a circular letter from Governor-General of the Philippines William Howard Taft, the newly formed Exposition Committee formally invited "all Army officers and officials of every Department and Bureau . . . down to the humblest one in Manila . . . to kindly join their efforts . . . in procuring superior exhibits which shall well represent the past and future as well as the actual state of economic and social development of the Philippines."[1] While many of the collected items focused specifically on economic development and procur ing "permanent profitable markets for natural resources," the centerpiece of the Philippine display was undoubtedly its "live exhibits."[2]

The Louisiana Purchase Exposition was ultimately an exercise in comprehensive, universal representation. Director of Exhibits Frederick J. V. Skiff envisioned a "modern universal exposition," "an encyclopedia of society," which constituted "a classified, compact, indexed compendium—available for ready reference—of the achievements and ideas of society."[3] The exposition was designed to vividly depict a compelling narrative of human evolution. While much of the academic literature on the subject has analyzed this exhibitionary narrative in terms of racial taxonomies, the display was fundamentally designed to present a much more malleable discourse of fractured and varied cultural progress.[4]

In 1899 the director of the Bureau of American Ethnology, William John McGee, published a landmark article in *American Anthropologist* entitled "The Trend of Human Progress." Building on the works of Lewis Henry Morgan, McGee argued for a more culturally based analysis of racial difference.[5] "While every anthropologist now recognizes the bestial ancestry of mankind," McGee wrote, "the increasing capacity of the cranium, and other features pertaining to the biotic development of the human body, there are some who have not yet been led to note the concomitant and much more significant demotic development of intellectual man." It was this notion of "demotic development" that ultimately underpinned McGee's theories of human difference. Classifying the world's disparate inhabitants "in terms of what they *do* rather than what they merely *are*" allowed for a much more nuanced and dynamic discourse of human evolution. Most importantly, it affirmed the possibility of effective forms of tutelary colonialism. Strict taxonomies of biotic race created an intranscendable gulf between Anglo-Saxon colonizers and their colonial subjects, thus negating much of the high-minded socially progressive ideals that American empire sought to impose and exhibit at the St. Louis World's Fair. Rather, McGee advocated an alternative taxonomy of human populations, "conveniently grouped in the four culture grades of savagery, barbarism, civilization, and enlightenment."[6] Five years after this publication McGee had the opportunity to implement his organizational matrix at the Louisiana Purchase Exposition as chief of the Department of Anthropology. Under his direction all "live exhibits" were filed neatly according to an evolutionary spectrum of human culture and society. Perhaps the most concise and vivid illustration of this organization was provided by the eleven hundred members of the Philippines Village.

When Americans seized the Philippines at the end of the nineteenth century, they were immediately struck by the islands' immense ethnic variety. Curious ethnologists, it seemed, had found a rich archive of human social and cultural development, comprising a vast spectrum of theoretical representativeness. "The study of the races of man is always of great interest," stated a Philippine Commission Report. "This is especially true in the Philippines, where live the most distinct people, representing the greater part of the races of the globe, in some instances pure, in others mixed since very remote times. Here man presents himself with the greatest variety of characteristics conceivable, as has been noted by eminent ethnologists . . . all the races are represented in these islands."[7] The Philippines thus embodied the critical principles of representativeness and extrapolation. The American exhibit at the Philippine Village could thus conceivably comprehend all other ethnological exhibits at the fair, making manifest the full spectrum from savagery to enlightenment. However, despite the supposedly comprehensive nature of the Philippine display, the exhibit was ultimately called upon to serve two sometimes divergent scientific and pedagogical functions.

On the one hand, the Philippine Village was a self-contained exhibit, set apart as an inclusive continuum of indigenous types ranging from the "head-hunting," "dog-eating," savage Igorots to the highly civilized Philippine Scouts and Constabulary. By viewing these communities in quick successive comparison, onlookers could draw broad lessons from the "demotic" differences in dress, materials, cultural customs, and habits. The Philippine exhibit inhabited a publicly and epistemologically demarcated space. It resided within a "museological modality,"[8] clearly designating "the cognitive position ascribed to the visitors," which was "assumed to be situated high above the world they gaze[d] upon." In this sense the Filipinos embodied the "principle of representativeness rather than that of rarity."[9] They stood in for an abstract notion of the human subject in general. As Tony Bennett explains in *The Birth of the Museum*, the staggering global heterogeneity of the nineteenth century convinced observers that "Man's unity [could] no longer be regarded as pre-given." Difference demanded an accounting. Ethnographic displays and museums "allowed that unity to be reconstituted in the construction of 'Man' as a project to be completed through time." It was an effort "to put back together the badly shattered human subject" as an object of academic study.[10] The Filipinos, as such objects, were meant to take on a kind of distant silence. Their position as an abstract representation clouded their proximity to fairgoers and relegated their presence at the exposition to a kind of sterile academic discourse, acknowledging the variety among themselves but casting that variety as an object of observation rather than participation. Nicholas Thomas explains the methodology as follows:

> Depiction and documentation—through such media as colonial reports and artifact collections as well as actual painting, drawing and photography [one might also add the reproduction of native art forms such as dance and theater]—did not merely create representations that were secondary to practices and realities, but constituted political actualities in themselves. Travelers and colonists could regard a space and another society, not as a geographic tract, nor an array of practices and relations, but as a thing depicted or described, that was immediately subject to their gaze. Other peoples, cultures and cities could thus be subsumed to the form of a picture, and seeing a thing first as a representation and secondly as something beyond a representation created a peculiar sense of power on the side of the viewing colonist.[11]

This Philippine Village was thus a display—a live diorama that allowed fair patrons to observe a contained arrangement of information comprehensively representative of a larger whole.

On the other hand, the Philippine exhibit was also meant to be an interactive display promoting a sense of otherization and cultural affirmation. The Filipinos, along with other live examples of varying grades of barbarism and savagery, were meant to create a stark binary between observers and the observed. "The special object of the Department of Anthropology is to show each half of the world how the other half lives," declared McGee in 1904.[12] These words were later echoed extensively in articles and souvenir guides and by the president of the Louisiana Purchase Exposition, David R. Francis.[13] The "great progress of the world was shown by striking contrasts," Francis explained in his memoir of the fair. "The exhibit of the department of Anthropology did much to indicate to our half of the world how the other half lives."[14] This "juxtaposition of 'savagery' and 'civilization'" has been a much noted aspect of the exposition.[15] Scholars such as Eric Breitbart, Raymond Corbey, and Tony Bennett have produced detailed examinations of the "large-scale representations of middle-class Selves and savage Others," which ultimately affirmed metropolitan societies' location at "the very pinnacle of the exhibitionary order of things."[16] Although observers at the fair theoretically participated in the grand narrative of human biotic and demotic evolution, their position was yet removed from the exhibits they viewed. The displays, in coordination with those who observed them, created "a single narrative which posits modern Man . . . as the outcome and, in some cases, telos of these processes."[17] John Schrecker insightfully describes this elevated view as "transcendent progress," or the notion that modern American society was "freeing itself from history, transcending it, and was entering an entirely new stage of human development, one that would be totally unencumbered by the problems and evils of the past."[18]

This binary function of the displays has led some scholars to view the Louisiana Purchase exhibits as "triumphs of hegemony," which "propagated the ideas and values of the country's political, financial, corporate, and intellectual leaders." According to this view, the exposition "offered millions of fairgoers an opportunity to reaffirm their collective national identity in an updated synthesis of progress and white supremacy that suffused the blueprints of future perfection offered by the fairs."[19] In this way, the exposition is viewed as a hegemonic "bourgeois fantasy world" and a "phenomenon of industrial capitalism."[20] The highly structured binary between observer and observed attempted to create a "cultural technology" designed to "shape the moral, mental and behaviourial characteristics of the population."[21] These assumptions are certainly in line with Edward Said's notions of a hegemonic Orientalist discourse. "The Orientalist," he argued in 1979, "is outside the Orient, both as an existential and as a moral fact. The principal product of this exteriority is of course representation."[22] This argument assumes, as have some scholars' work on the exposition, that the pervasive hegemony of Orientalist representation was by and large passively accepted by those within the dominant culture as well as by those being represented. As Martha Clevenger asserted in her collection of fair accounts, "visitors did not fundamentally disagree with or question the world view of the Fair planners."[23]

Much of the recent scholarship in what has been termed "New Imperial History" has significantly problematized these notions of hegemony, however. Scholars such as Ann Laura Stoler and Frederick Cooper, Nicholas Thomas, Craig Reynolds, Tony Day, Vicente Rafael, Reynaldo Ileto, Paul Kramer, and Patricio Abinales have provided significantly disaggregated examinations of empire that vividly demonstrate the muddled contact zones of contestation, contingency, and negotiation.[24] Rather than relying on analytical models of antagonistic binaries or hegemonic colonial entities, this school of thought has advocated examining "metropole and colony in a single analytic field, addressing the weight one gives to causal connections and the primacy of agency in its different parts."[25]

Although it is tempting to treat colonial expositions as an exception to these ideas because the encounter occurs in the metropole rather than in the colony, awash in the culture and societal structures of the colonizers, expositions are indeed among the best historical examples of the colonies' perpetual ability to "talk back."[26] The intimate proximity of the colonized to a massive audience in the metropole enhanced rather than diminished their ability to contest, subvert, negotiate, and ultimately remake imperial discourse on their own terms. This was sometimes accomplished through resistance but more often than not through selective collaboration. The most interesting aspect of colonial display in the Philippine Village was the manner in which the "live exhibits" embodied their ascribed roles in unexpected ways. The exhibited subjects were often the more keen observers, deftly recognizing trends, expectations, and opportunities to enhance their own positions of power. This book examines a particularly soft spot in the subjective and contested colonial discourse between colonizer and colonized at the Louisiana Purchase Exposition—that of the Philippine Muslims, also known as Moros.[27]

The Moro Exhibit

When American military personnel arrived in Mindanao and the Sulu Archipelago in 1899, Filipino Muslims numbered approximately three hundred thousand.[28] Although American imperialists frequently referred to their Muslim subjects as "Moros" generally, there were at least thirteen distinct ethnolinguistic groups inhabiting Mindanao and its satellite islands that identified as Muslim. These were Tao Sug (Tausug), Maranao, Maguindanao, Samal, Yakan, Jama, Mapun, Palawan, Molbog, Kalagan, Kalibugan, Sangil, and Badjao. Colonial authorities sometimes acknowledged these distinctions but typically treated the Moros as a relatively homogeneous population in terms of colonial policy and organization.

Islam first arrived in the Sulu Archipelago via trade in the late fourteenth century. The first significant Muslim presence in the southern Philippines is attributed to Makdum Ibrahim Al-Akbar, a Muslim merchant and missionary from Malacca who eventually settled in the Sulu archipelago. Al-Akbar's efforts were followed by a number of Islamic pioneers who pressed further into the archipelago. The most notable of these was

Abu Bak'r, a reported native of Mecca who standardized Islamic practice throughout the sultanate by introducing Arabic language and script, the Koran, Islamic legal systems, and Mosque culture.[29] According to tradition, Abu Bak'r's reign as the sultan of Sulu in the early fifteenth century is generally considered to be the formative period of Islamicization. Although missionary contact with mainland Mindanao was certainly probable during these early phases of Islamicization, the formal introduction of Islam to Mindanao is historically attributed to Sharif Muhammad Kabungsuwan who established a permanent Muslim settlement near Cotabato. While the past century has witnessed a great deal of romantic mythologizing concerning the spread of Islam in the Philippines, the general time frames and processes of Islamicization above are generally accepted.

Early Muslim missionary merchants such as Abu Bak'r and others brought a syncretic brand of Sufi (mystical) Sunnah (Sunni) Islam to the southern Philippines that had developed through a myriad of intercultural fusions throughout the region. As Sufism filtered through India and into Southeast Asia it developed an informal system of oral transmission through traveling teachers and mystics who demonstrated their deeper knowledge of Islam through miraculous healings, prophesies, and other spiritual manifestations.[30] Despite Sufism's debatable syncretisms, Islamic foundations—such as a deep reverence for the Koran, the words of the Prophet Mohammad (Hadith), and various aspects of Shari'ah Law—became firmly rooted in Moro tradition and framed their identities for centuries before Western contact.[31]

While Luzon and the Visayas succumbed to Spanish colonialism in the sixteenth century, Moros successfully resisted Hispanization for the next three hundred years. Only after 1848 and the advent of mechanized gunboats were the Spanish able to establish a sustained presence in Mindanao and Sulu. Even by 1896, however, Spain's suzerainty was nominal at best with only a few garrisoned outposts in Jolo, Siasi, Bongao, Marawi, and Cotabato.[32] Despite its limited territorial impact, the Spanish colonial period is largely regarded as a sustained genocidal war on Islam, which continues to echo today.[33]

Following the chaotic and bloody withdrawal of the Spanish forces from their southern posts in 1899 after Spain's defeat to the Americans, the United States inherited a virtually autonomous collection of Muslim tribes largely undisturbed by Western imperialism. Lacking any effective

colonial infrastructure, Americans neutralized the Moro threat by grant-
ing provisional autonomy and guaranteeing religious freedom through the
Bates Treaty. Signed by Jamal-ul Kiram, sultan of Sulu, and other minor
datus, the treaty allowed American military forces to occupy Muslim areas
without expanding the broader insurgency conflict raging in the north. On
October 30, 1899, Mindanao, the Sulu Archipelago, and Palawan became
the "Military District of Mindanao and Jolo," formally inaugurating
American military rule in the southern Philippines.

While the Bates Treaty succeeded in its original objective of maintaining
peace in Mindanao, by 1903 many aspects of the treaty had become politically untenable. American noninterference with Moro slavery in particular
prompted strong calls for colonial authorities to abrogate the treaty and
institute full colonial government in the Military District. By July of that
year colonial officials eagerly set about instituting full American authority
by reorganizing the Military District into a government entity known as
Moro Province. President Theodore Roosevelt formally abrogated the Bates
Treaty less than a year later, on March 2, 1904. Noncompliance among
Muslim leaders served as the official rationale. From 1903 to 1913 Moro
Province provided a separate and nearly autonomous military colonial
regime. Although officially accountable to the Philippine Commission and
structurally part of the colonial regime at large, military leaders in Moro
Province enjoyed tremendous autonomy and conducted their imperial policies with very little interference. Unencumbered by the competing interests
and political maneuverings characteristic of civilian government in the
north, only a small contingent of administrators governed Moro Province
with remarkable coherence and efficiency. As a subset of the larger colonial
apparatus, Moros were governed as "wild peoples"—a distinction applied
to those who fell outside the Hispanizing and Christianizing influences
of Spanish colonialism. Yet, even within the subset of "wild peoples,"
American administrators carefully recognized varying degrees of civilization and culture, which produced a ranked hierarchy of the "uncivilized."

With the formalization of military rule in Mindanao and Sulu, both
military and civilian officials in the Philippines were eager to organize a
detailed Moro exhibit for the Louisiana Purchase Exposition. The St. Louis
display was to represent the culmination of nearly five years of intensive
ethnological studies in the southern Philippines. From the very beginning
of formal colonization, ethnologists and officials started pursuing a vast

scholarly project to discover, catalogue, exhibit, and govern the Philippines' Muslim South. Much of this impulse derived from a desire to rectify and atone for the poor management and abuse of Native Americans. Anthropologists such as Daniel Brinton urged US officials to make ethnology a foundational aspect of policy formation in the Philippines. "It behooves us," wrote Brinton in 1899, "to give [Filipinos] that scientific investigation which alone can afford a true guide to their proper management."[34] Many colonial officials agreed, citing past mistakes in the governance of Native Americans. "There is no doubt," suggested in a Philippine Commission Report, "that if careful ethnologic work had been undertaken and carried on among the Indians in the early days of the Republic many mistakes which have been made might have been avoided."[35] Consequently, in 1901 the Philippine Commission created the Bureau of Non-Christian Tribes. The bureau's mission was overtly ethnological and scholarly in scope, as laid out in Act No. 253 of the Philippine Commission:

[The Bureau of Non-Christian Tribes is to] conduct systematic investigation with reference to non-Christian tribes of the Philippine Islands, in order to ascertain the name of its tribe, the limits of its territory which it occupies, the approximate number of individuals which compose it, their social organizations and their languages, beliefs, manners, and customs, with special view to determining the most practicable means for bringing about their advancement in civilization and material prosperity.[36]

Two years later, in 1903, the Philippine Commission enhanced the bureau's focus via official act by renaming it the "Ethnological Survey of the Philippine Islands" with instructions to carry out "systematic researches on anthropology and ethnology among all the inhabitants of the Philippine Islands."[37] Ethnological studies and accounts soon became the dominant theme in commission reports, censuses, and news articles in both metropole and colony. Officials were greatly pleased with the results, particularly in Mindanao and Sulu. An article in the 1904 Philippine Commission Report happily noted "that the work of the [ethnological] survey will prove itself to be not merely scientifically valuable, but practically useful in the work of controlling and assisting . . . the uncivilized people of the islands."[38]

More than governance, however, many American colonialists began to see an inherent value in preserving and exhibiting Moro culture. Through discovery, Americans felt that Mindanao and Sulu's material and cultural past was becoming part of a world heritage. By the time of the Louisiana Purchase Exposition there was a persistent call among government officials and ethnologists to formally curate Moro culture. For example, Acting Chief for the Secretary of the Interior in the Philippines Merton Miller argued that the "time is especially favorable now for building up a museum of ethnology because the great museums of the United States and Europe have not yet begun to make collections from the islands. When these museums have once begun collecting, the prices of many things will rise and it will be increasingly difficult to get them at any price."[39] Moro culture had value, and the world was about to witness it.

On December 1, 1903, an agent named Frederick Lewis secured a contract with the Insular Government of the Philippines to collect and manage an exhibit of Samal Moros from Zamboanga. He desired "a representative group of Samal Moros to engage in their daily pursuits while in attendance on the Exposition, and a collection of their arms and household effects"; "a characteristic display" including "weapons, fishing gear, mats, native fabrics, wearing apparel, raw material, and other requisites." With help from Datu Facundo, the brother of the powerful Samal headman and staunch American ally Datu Rajah Muda Mandi, Lewis was able to persuade a group of forty Moros to attend the exhibit.[40] Including Datu Facundo, there were nineteen men, eleven women, five boys, and five girls. The assemblage soon joined another contingent of forty Lanao Moros in Manila who were acquired and managed by Charles H. Wax. The combined groups quickly organized and performed a number of minor exhibitions for colonial officials and curious observers in Manila, which "attracted considerable attention." The brief training period was also designed to acculturate Moros to "the ways of modern civilization" as they prepared for their trip to the metropole. Both Lewis and Wax operated under strict governmental surveillance and reporting. Although private agents were allowed to facilitate the acquisition and organization of displays, the colonial regime was explicit that "Nobody is authorized to collect exhibits of the Philippine Islands for the St. Louis Exposition without the knowledge and consent of the Philippine Exposition Board in Manila." All exhibits, whether material or live, had to be formally divided into 15 departments, 114 groups, 807 classes, and identified with at least 35 separate descriptions.[41] Most importantly, however, acquired exhibits must be "shown to the best possible advantage."[42]

Upon their arrival in St. Louis the Moros immediately began salaried work constructing a series of so-called native houses. Each structure was composed entirely of "bamboo, nipa, and rattan" with "no nails or other material entering into the construction of the dwellings." Fair organizers felt it was essential that the village represented "the work of the men of the village, and theirs alone," so as to authentically convey the Moros' "own peculiar ideas and style of architecture." Both the Samal and Lanao dwellings resided on the shores of an artificial body of water called Arrowhead Lake. As in the construction of the homes, authenticity was paramount. The shoreline "was covered with sand and gravel in an attempt to reproduce the sea beach as nearly as possible, the result being fairly satisfactory and realistic." In addition to their domiciles, the Moros also constructed an administration building, which served as a museum for cultural artifacts, and two theaters for various cultural performances. Original designs called for separate Samal and Lanao villages so that each "should constitute an exhibit in itself." It was soon "deemed advisable," however, to consolidate

Fig. I.1. Moro residences over Arrowhead Lake in the Moro Village

the two groups into a unitary "Moro Village," though the architectural styles and cultural performances remained distinct.[43]

On June 18, 1904, the Moro Village officially opened to the public. All eighty of the "live exhibits" followed a highly scripted program designed to thoroughly demonstrate authentic Moro life. Patrons were privy to the intimacy of "daily home life, dwellings, [and] household furnishing." Moros engaged in a variety of "native industries and occupations," including pearl polishing, weaving, braiding mats, and fishing in Arrowhead Lake with native boats and fishing tackle. Cultural dances occurred at "stated intervals throughout the day." Native music was "rendered continuously from the opening to the closing hour." Even unscripted recreation was essential to the display. Children were of particular interest as they "disported themselves in their boats and in the water from morning to night." Lewis and Wax strove to ensure that every aspect of Moro life remained transparent and remarkable. "Every possible attraction was introduced that might prove interesting and instructive to visitors to the village," reported the Philippine Commission.[44]

Fig. I.2. Samal Moro musicians with their instruments in the Moro Village

By creating the Moro exhibit in this particular way, fair organizers and colonial officials participated in a deeply established "pedagogy of imperial anthropology."[45] The Moro Village was constructed to effectively commodify and exoticize the mundane aspects of Moro life.[46] The passive existence of "authentic" subjects was then punctuated by sensational and fantastic demonstrations of controlled savage violence and repugnant social practices meant to shock and titillate the viewing public. It was critical that fair patrons believed that Moro activities were "being done rather than represented" to create the "illusion of authenticity or realness."[47] This created a tenuous and ultimately untenable balance in which colonial authorities sought to scrub any imperial influence from the display so as to affirm its authenticity, while simultaneously maintaining the exhibitionary imperative that such an exotic society could only be "understood within the cultural logic of . . . colonial empire."[48] These divergent objects were particularly vulnerable in the Moro Village where live exhibits inhabited the ambiguous and unsettled category of "semi-civilized," leaving a wide latitude for varying impressions and unintended messages.

The Ambivalence of Semi-Civilized

Moro contributions to the Philippine exhibit at the Louisiana Purchase Exposition have been largely obscured by other aspects of the Philippine display. Although the Moro Village attracted a considerable amount of attention in local and national media outlets at the time, it has since faded from scholarly and popular historical consciousness. In this book I seek to revive and contextualize Moro participation in the exposition, not as a historical footnote to more apparent manifestations of empire but as a critical window into the nuanced and surprisingly textured nature of American imperial discourse. I argue that the Moro display provided a distinctive liminal space in the dialectical relationship between civilization and savagery. The Moros embodied a living "contact zone" where the various discursive formations of "colonizer" and "colonized"— "center" and "periphery," "civilized" and "savage"—could be negotiated and contested by either side. Ethnography, as the primary intellectual discourse of empire at the fair, was both "allegorical" and "autobiographic," requiring a deep level of mutual recognition and participation from all participants.[49] In this way, the Moros provided a kind of transcultural bridge. Through their nondescript designation as "semi-civilized," they undermined and mediated the various binaries structuring the exposition. In this book I seek to tease out the internal logic of this mediation.

American ideological and intellectual engagement with the Philippine exhibit was largely circumscribed by imposing binaries at either end of the evolutionary spectrum. The "savage" Igorot and Aeta (Negrito) subjects represented a clear antithesis to American modernity and civilization. The wild and shocking nature of the savage displays repeatedly affirmed American conceptions of white middle-class dominance buttressed by the material trappings of industrial modernity. It presented observers with a dialectical construction of both object and subject meant to "form and shape the moral, mental and behaviourial characteristics of the population."[50] The binary of civilization and savagery at the Philippine exhibit was a cultural technology of tutelary empire meant to educate members of the metropole rather than those of the colony. The apparent lack of clothing, technology, sanitation, political culture, and institutionalized religions among the primitives stood in stark contrast to "the bourgeois fantasy world" of abundance demonstrated at the fair, affirming the notion that "the real importance of the Philippines to the United States has been moral and exemplary rather than strategic or economic."[51] The viewing public was encouraged to conform to modern standards of civility and taste by moving away from their antithesis.

At the other end of the evolutionary spectrum, American patrons faced a somewhat more complex binary in the form of "civilized" Filipinos. In order to demonstrate the power of tutelary colonialism, a provisional battalion of Philippine Scouts and members of the Philippine Constabulary figured prominently in the display. Dressed in tidy well-pressed uniforms, Filipino soldiers entertained crowds by marching, drilling, saluting, and offering patriotic anthems played by a brass band. They passed among the fairgoers as foreign visitors, mingling at gatherings, attending luncheons and honorary dinners, and for a short time residing at the Hamilton Hotel in St. Louis.[52] Yet, despite the behaviors and symbols of civilization that were immediately recognizable to exposition visitors, the Philippine soldiers bore an unmistakable stigma of "colonial mimicry." These civilized colonial subjects embodied Homi Bhabha's ambivalent category of "almost the same, but not quite," provoking "a process of disavowal" and the colonial cringe of inappropriate proximity. "Civilized" Filipinos' proximate subjectivity had the unsettling effect of affirming colonial tutelage while simultaneously producing a menace capable of disrupting social and racial norms. Bhabha's trenchant observation, that "to be Anglicized is emphatically not to be English" can be aptly translated to the civilized Filipinos' "Americanization" at the exposition.[53] This process of disavowal created a polar gap between observers and exhibits that was, in many cases, more virulent and lasting than the markers of savagery. In this case, white middle-class American civilization was again affirmed by a more proximate but inauthentic replication of itself. The true article became more acutely apparent as it stood side by side with its counterfeit, the civilized Filipino. The intranscendable distance between colonizer and colonized maintained its structure and efficacy through this veiled binary.[54]

The Moros, however, provided a middle ground. Officially designated as "semi-civilized," Filipino Muslims represented an unexpectedly welcomed mediation and challenge to the binary logic and discomfort of the exposition. They occupied an ambiguous interstitial space in an otherwise rigid colonial discourse of race and empire by simultaneously embodying the characteristics of opposing binaries. The Moros could, at various times, be cast as both colonizer and colonized, civilized and savage, advanced and primitive, good and evil, beautiful and ugly, or human and bestial. They bore a distinct hybridity and a complexity characterized by deep ambivalence. However, unlike Bhabha's classical ambivalence, the Moros did not provoke the same unsettling implications for colonial rule.[55]

Rather, the Moros' ambiguous status was curiously embraced by American patrons and the press as a malleable subjectivity, sensitive and attentive to the vagaries of an evolving colonial discourse. Moros were, at one moment, cast as bloodthirsty savages, pirates, and warriors with a romantic sensationalism rivaling that of dime-store novels. The next moment they appeared as proto-Americans, exemplifying the rugged individualism, frontier masculinity, and endangered homespun values seemingly threatened by technical modernity. In the first case there seemed to be no fundamental fear of violence, only a kind of wistful curiosity; a desire to vicariously indulge in the now forbidden practices and desires of bygone eras. In the second case, unlike the Philippine Constabulary and Scouts, Moro mimicry was tolerated as a positive sign of colonial tutelage without the discomfort of comparative mockery. The ever-present residual signs of Moro savagery marked a temporal and cultural distance, ameliorating the proximity by contextualizing Moro mimicry into a romantic American past rather than a tenuous present. In this way both sides of the colonial divide were implicated in a discursive ambivalence as they engaged one another to create stories about themselves at the fair.

The Moros' appeal as "semi-civilized" exhibits cast a wide net among the highly variegated visitors to the exposition. While much of the historical literature has tended to "Occidentalize" fairgoers as an undifferentiated stream of imperial observers, fair organizers were much more acutely aware of the socioeconomic and racial range of their patrons.[56] In keeping with the Progressive Era values and pedagogies of public refinement, American elites hoped that educational opportunities would "diminish the appeal of the tavern" and increase "the sobriety and industriousness of the populace." Museums, expositions, public lectures, and other programs were meant to assimilate the lower classes into a homogeneous "bourgeois public sphere" and incorporate them within "a programme of progressive self-improvement."[57] William McGee, chief of the Department of Anthropology of the Louisiana Purchase Exposition, dubbed his exhibit a "university of the masses" with "the special object . . . to show each half of the world how the other half lives."[58] William F. Burdell, president of the Ohio Commission to the World's Fair, similarly claimed that "a month's visit to the World's Fair is worth more than a year at college, and for anyone four weeks of serious inquiry and sight-seeing here is easily the equivalent of two years of general travel over the world."[59] However, such valuable and thick instruction was only a benefit to those "capable of appreciating it." The "mass of visitors, unless [the exhibit's] object is explained, learn little from it except what is taken in by the eye," argued a writer for the *World's Fair Bulletin.* "Even people well informed within the range of their observation or study will see at the World's Fair much [that] will be . . . incomprehensible to them."[60] Thus, the exposition required careful guidance lest observers engage in treacherous misinterpretations and arrive at false conclusions regarding the benefits of modernity and the perils of the past. Organizers had to "devise ways of regulating the [intellectual] conduct of their visitors."[61] The exhibits were consequently designed to project a certain intellectual authority over those who observed them by placing patrons at a perpetual epistemic disadvantage. Ivan Karp explains the methodology:

Almost by definition, audiences do not bring to exhibitions the full range of cultural resources necessary for comprehending them; otherwise there would be no point to exhibiting. Audiences are left with two choices: either they define their experience of the exhibition to fit with their existing categories of knowledge, or they reorganize their categories to fit better with their experience. Ideally, it is the shock of nonrecognition that enables the audience to choose the latter alternative. The challenge for exhibition makers is to provide within exhibitions the contexts and resources that enable audiences to choose to reorganize their knowledge.[62]

The exoticism and foreignness of the Philippine exhibit was intended to automatically disable qualified interpretations by the viewing public. As Steven Lavine has observed, exhibited objects derive their "significance as corroborative evidence."[63] Colonial exhibits serve a purpose only inasmuch as they corroborate and support established truths and narratives. Without these preexisting backdrops, colonial artifacts—both living and nonliving—risked floating freely in an ocean of vague interpretation. The exhibits, then, exist within a tenuous social contract, "a socially agreed-upon reality that exists only as long as confidence in the voice of the exhibition holds."[64]

But what if the "shock of nonrecognition" fails to shake the world-view of the visitors? What if fair patrons refuse to participate in the exhibit's social contract and instead subtly derive unintended messages from the display? What occurs when observers see beyond the sensational exoticism of the subjects and instead connect with a shared experience of temporal dislocation within modernity? It must be remembered that a large majority of fairgoers were themselves "pre-modern." As Eric Breitbart points out: "In spite of America's urbanization, many, if not most, of the fair's visitors lived on farms or in small towns; their conception of time and space was anchored in an agricultural, not an industrial framework." Many visitors had never beheld electric lights, much less the mechanical engines of industry.[65] In this sense both the Moros and rural Americans experienced the World's Fair in similar ways. They both came from analogous technological circumstances. Their sense of space, time, kinship, and connection to the earth was firmly rooted in premodern modes of living. They were both offered "a paradigm for the experience of modernity" that sought to hasten sociocultural evolution and homogenize them into the bourgeois cultural of industrial modernity.[66] Therefore, the "shock of nonrecognition" applied as much to the wonders of technical modernity as it did to the exoticism of the Moros. Both Moros and rural American patrons shared a certain kinship in this, which was manifested in public discourses in the local press. The constructed binary of colonizer and colonized was subverted by this shared experience and resulted in subtle forms of recognition.

As a living conduit representing both the past and the present, the Moros also had tremendous appeal for those who were fully rooted within industrial modernity. There is an immense body of literature exploring the particulars of the United States' uncertain and unresolved relationship with modern life. The intense psychosocial crisis afflicting bourgeois Americans in the late nineteenth and early twentieth centuries presented with such severity as to leave virtually no aspect of traditional life undisturbed. Historical notions of family, gender, religion, locality, labor, consumption, community, time, and religious belief were suddenly and violently displaced, altered, or disenchanted by the clinical sterility of modern science and the dubious reality of an anomalously manufactured world. T. J. Jackson Lears describes the malaise as "a sense of moral impotence and spiritual sterility—a feeling that life had become not only over-civilized but also curiously unreal."[67] Burdened with the "diffuse fatigue" of a secular, materialistic, and banal modernity, "Americans began to imagine a self that was neither simple nor genuine, but fragmented and socially constructed."[68] Identities became codified and flattened in a number of intersecting serialities, without regard to individuality or autonomous selfhood.[69] Many Americans responded to these feelings by slipping "into immobilizing, self-punishing depressions"—the most notable and widespread of which was known as "neurasthenia" or "nervous prostration."[70] Characterized by a "paralysis of will" and an acute detachment from "real life," neurasthenia ravaged the American bourgeoisie with new modern terrors.[71] Educated, professional populations in metropolitan areas were especially susceptible to this severe form of nervous prostration, which confirmed neurasthenia as "a product of overcivilization."[72] These disruptions left bourgeois Americans yearning for a connection to romantic histories and lost modes of living.[73]

Hence, one of the most attractive, yet unexpected, aspects of the fair was the "insatiable demands of nostalgia."[74] While the exposition was meant to provide a clearly progressive historical and conceptual map to modernity, scholars such as Martha Clevenger have found that the "bulk of the Fair visitors' narratives . . . illustrate how the Fair engendered its own immediate nostalgia."[75] Exposition patrons sought out the past as much as the future as they attempted to locate themselves within the chaotic temporal milieu heaving about them. As Chester Starr explains, modern temporal insecurities often produce "the sense of a reversal of time, as generations seek to revivify an earlier isolation or simpler ways; even when they are not successful, they often walk backward into the future."[76]

This was certainly Theodore Roosevelt's tone in his dedicatory speech of the exposition on April 30, 1903. While Roosevelt paid token reverence to the achievements of industrial modernity, his overall speech was consumed with a kind of melancholy nostalgia. The old settlers of the Louisiana Purchase, he argued, were "picked out by a process of natural selection from among the most enterprising individuals of the nations of Western Europe." In an effusive tribute he then lauded the "aggressive and masterful character of the hardy pioneer folk," who were "mighty in war" and "mighty in strength to tame the rugged wilderness," who embodied "the qualities of self-mastery and self-restraint" as well as the "great fighting virtues" that allowed them to "overcome the forces of hostile men and hostile nature." And while the general progressive spirit of the exposition would seem to celebrate the passing of those difficult days into the material comfort of modern America, Roosevelt lamented it. "The old pioneer days are gone," he mourned. "The peculiar frontier conditions have vanished" and, along with them, "their roughness and their hardship, their incredible toil and their *wild, half-savage romance*" (italics added). Nevertheless, a return to the technological, economic, and material deprivation of the "old pioneer days" was not only impossible, it was antithetical to the entire purpose of the exposition. Roosevelt, like so many other Americans, attempted to stake out a vague and ambivalent middle ground, wedding the ideals of the past with the manufactured, impersonal, industrial circumstances of the present. The "manliness and stalwart hardihood of the frontiersmen can be given even freer scope under the conditions surrounding the complex industrialism of the present day," he encouraged. "The old days were great because the men who lived in them had mighty qualities; and we must make the new days great by showing the same qualities."[77] How this could be done, he left largely unanswered.

Roosevelt's ambivalence regarding the transformative and totalizing effects of modernity reveal a profound countercurrent of both thought and discourse that undermined large parts of the exposition. Although humanity's historical heritage was certainly celebrated and commemorated throughout the festivities, the exposition was ultimately structured to discredit the past. Despite this purpose, neither fair patrons nor fair organizers agreed to fully participate. Both sought a kind of hybrid synthesis of temporalities; a state of temporal transcendence allowing them to straddle the old and the new in a moment of historical transition.

This sense of temporal duality lay at the heart of American fascination with Moros at the exposition. The Moros' designation as "semi-civilized" appealed to the "wild, half-savage romance" that was thought to characterize the United States' unique ascent into modernity. This designation recalled a particularly quixotic notion of American frontier masculinity that was increasingly endangered by industrial comforts. The Moros' hyphenated limbo also placed them at the precipice of a great, familiar transition into modernity; it implied tremendous potential for profound colonial success, thus affirming the tutelary power of American empire. The Moros thus simultaneously embodied a nostalgic vision of a waning past and a hopeful ascent into a progressive future. Americans saw themselves in the living exhibits at the Moro Village.

The American Orientalist gaze was not simply one way, however. The Moros did not simply take up residence at the fair as inanimate artifacts awaiting interpretation. Other scholars have strongly argued that displayed subjects were not categorical victims but, rather, exercised a great deal of agency by participating in the exposition on their own terms.[78] The Moros certainly fit this description. It must be remembered that live exhibits were recruited, engaged in negotiations, were paid salaries, and exercised a great deal of influence on the ways in which they were displayed and how that display interacted with the public. Adventure, economic opportunity, access to power, and enhancing one's prestige within colonial society were all powerful motivators, among others, to participate in the exposition. Although American patrons saw strong elements of themselves in their exhibits at the Moro Village, these impressions did not spawn solely from their own imaginations. Moros were keen observers of American attitudes and tastes and shrewdly crafted their public personae to fit popular expectations and desires. In this way the construction of Moro subjects at the fair was not only collaborative and discursive, but was often dictated by the Moros themselves, who held a certain epistemological advantage over an impressionable, receptive public. Fair-goers were actively seeking an extraordinary experience. Exhibit organizers framed it, but ultimately, it was the Moros who provided it. And therein lay a tremendous amount of power.

Note on Sources

One of the well-known difficulties in examining the experiences of subaltern colonial subjects is a glaring lack of indigenously crafted sources. The vast majority of colonial histories are derived from records produced by the powers that be, and they contain a distinct and unabashed bias in favor of colonial policies and objectives current at the time. Indigenous voices are rarely given priority and are often excluded entirely. This presents a particularly difficult dilemma for scholars. The evidentiary requirements of a strict empirical analysis of colonial histories necessarily renders subaltern subjects invisible—or at most, passive—two-dimensional objects taking part in someone else's history. For many historians, myself included, this is simply unacceptable. Hence, in this book I employ a method of discourse analysis to coax Moro voices from non-Moro sources. Given the unfortunate lack of subaltern materials available from the fair, I seek to conjure the voices of the colonized by reading against the grain, between the lines and by employing theories and strategies that are designed to make the subaltern heard within a history of ideas and discourse. In this sense I openly employ and advocate a "Foucaultian sense" of the term "archive," demonstrated by Edward Said as an "enunciated field" of colonial records collectively contributing to and crafting the subjective colony.[79]

The Moros provided a dimension to the Louisiana Purchase Exhibit that is critical to its understanding. The interplay between Moro subjects, other Filipino exhibits, fair organizers, and the American public reveals a stark analytical window into the mutually constitutive nature of metropolitan and colonial societies. This interplay discloses a complex and discursive exchange of symbols and ideas forming the respective subjectivities of colonizer and colonized in a surreal moment of colonial theater, played out in the unlikely setting of St. Louis, Missouri.

1

SENSATIONAL SAVAGES

From the outset the Moro display was plagued with a number of competing tensions. Fair organizers at large generally promoted the Philippine exhibit as a highly scientific endeavor designed to address the most pertinent academic questions of the day. The fact that many of the Philippine displays could be shocking and exotic was merely an enabling factor to the fundamental purposes of the exhibit. In report after report, exposition officials readily acknowledged the potentially sensational nature of the displays but immediately grounded them in "scientific value."[1] The "innate and intuitive curiosity which renders alien races so attractive" could be a powerful means of satisfying "the more serious impulses of students," particularly since "the United States has undertaken to civilize the natives of the Philippine islands."[2] Exposition President David R. Francis similarly affirmed the hierarchical purposes of the displays: "While popular, these interesting—some of them almost sensational—exhibits [have] a scientific base. . . . The assemblage of human types was not only a source of attraction but served serious ends. While gratifying the untrained curiosity which leads even the child to look with wonder on the alien, it satisfied also the intelligent observer that there is a course of progress running from lower to higher humanity."[3]

The sensational promotion of exotic live exhibits could serve as a kind of symbiotic pedagogical tool for educating the masses. Organizers could entice "lowbrow" audiences into a profoundly genuine educational experience by appealing to their desires for edgy entertainment. As Barbara Kirshenblatt-Gimblett explains, live exhibits tended "strongly in the direction of spectacle, blurring the line still further between morbid curiosity and scientific interest, chamber of horrors and medical exhibition, circus and zoological garden, theater and living ethnographic display." This was particularly important at a time when theaters, minstrel performances, circuses, and freak shows increasingly came under attack from conservative Protestant groups and high-minded social progressives as vulgar and degrading forms of entertainment. However, when such oddities and sexualized forms were presented in museums or exhibitions in the name of science, they were suddenly rendered acceptable and even desirable.[4]

This tension between sensationalism and scientific value was even more complex for colonial officials in the Philippines. Governor-General William H. Taft and the Exposition Board were explicit in 1902 that "in selecting the exhibits care must be taken that they are shown to the best possible advantage. . . . The purpose of the Philippine exhibit is not only to create interest and sympathy for the Philippine Islands, [but also] to give confidence in the intelligence and capacity of the natives."[5] Highlighting savagery, violence, and oddities were anathema to attracting potential American investment and settlement, particularly in Mindanao and Sulu. Sensational savagery was also distinctly repugnant to Filipino nationalists who were struggling to convince US policy makers and the American public of their modernity and capacity for self-rule. Senor Vicente Nepomuceno, a member of the Philippine honorary commission, blistered the exhibit in the local press, arguing that "the Moros, Negritos and Igorrotes" represented an insignificant minority of "backward and non-progressive races" that were in fact "rapidly dying out." He argued:

[Such exhibits] no more represent the people of the Philippines than the dying Indian represents the American people, and the Americans would resent such an exhibition far more vigorously than we have. . . . [T]he impression has gone abroad that we are barbarians. . . . The Filipino people are being preposterously misrepresented at the Fair. . . . [T]hey have gone into the remotest corners of the islands, gathered together the lowest types of the inhabitants and brought them to this country to exhibit in an attempt to justify their paternal grip on the islands.[6]

Colonial officials and Philippine exhibit organizers could not help but agree, much to their chagrin. The official *Souvenir of the Philippine Exposition* attempted to inform patrons that the "savage" exhibits "would be as much of a curiosity on the streets of Manila as on the streets of St. Louis" and that "it might be edifying, if not altogether interesting, . . . to learn something of the real Filipino."[7]

Looking back, colonial officials similarly questioned the manner in which the Philippine exhibit was presented. In the 1905 Report of the Philippine Exposition Board, officials offered a tepid critique but quickly absolved themselves of any responsibility for public misconceptions or charges of sensational exploitation: "Owing to a feeling that this topic [the various sensational characteristics and habits of the 'savage' exhibits] might safely be left to the thoughtful care of the political press, the advertising departments have avoided official mention of it and have endeavored to call attention to the more worthy characteristics of the natives." Nevertheless, although it "is not true that the savages have been unduly exploited at the expense of the more dignified exhibits, . . . no amount of emphasis on the commercial exhibits, Constabulary drills and Scouts parades has distracted attention from the 'dog-eaters' and 'head-hunters.'" And "to this fact," they concluded, "may be attributed no small part of the income of the Philippine Exposition."[8]

This last admission was, of course, the ultimate standard by which the exhibits would be judged. Much like the modern-day race for television ratings, exposition officials were determined to attract viewers by any means necessary. The directors of the Moro exhibit were unabashed in this regard. Their initial marketing efforts were characterized by tales of violence, savagery, heathenism, and depravity, all of which the local press was eager to disseminate in daily columns. However, following this initial phase of sensational fearmongering, exposition officials and the Moros themselves found that the public was drawn to their exhibit for other, unforeseen reasons.

The Moros stirred unexpected feelings of nostalgia in modern Americans. The Moro exhibit, as displayed, seemed to embody lost and exotic worlds of frontier masculinity and Orientalist fantasies. It presented a vicarious conduit through which bourgeois Americans could experience activities and modes of living now expressly forbidding in progressive modern America. In the expositional "world of simulated experience" and "simulated travel," the Philippines' Muslim South represented an exotic, yet nostalgically familiar destination where colonizer and colonized, object and subject, could engage in a mutually informed experience of cultural hybridity.[9] The liminal space of the "semi-civilized" Moros allowed Americans a way in and a way back to places they sought, while simultaneously providing Moros with access to sources and habitations of power in the always malleable discourse of American empire.

Marketing Savagery

Both Frederick Lewis and Charles Wax had little trouble building initial publicity for their exhibits in the Moro Village. By 1904 the various Muslim tribes of the southern Philippines had already found their way into the American press and carried a heavy reputation for savagery and violence. In the opening years of the twentieth century, articles appeared in newspapers and magazines across the country. The violence and volatility of the United States' newly acquired Muslim subjects provided a continual dramatic flair to its colonial frontier. Tales of cruelty, barbarism, religious fanaticism, and exotic sexuality titillated readers in columns throughout the country.[10]

The local press in St. Louis seized on these preexistent tropes in the days leading up to the exposition and ran them almost continuously after the Moros arrived. The *Argus* and the *St. Louis Post-Dispatch* boasted that the live Moro exhibits were no different from the "fanatical Mohammedans" who were butchering US servicemen in the Philippines. In early May 1904 the *St. Louis Post-Dispatch* cited a recent engagement in which seventeen US soldiers were killed and five wounded in Moro Province. "On the Philippine reservation . . . there are 120 savage Moros," the paper warned, "differing in no respect from those who . . . ambushed Company F. . . . The Moros are the most savage of the native tribes. . . . [they] are so treacherous that it is deemed unsafe for a stranger to go among them in the Cuartel unattended. . . . Their edged weapons are

Fig. 1.1. A Moro family

The three
Sultans
Ambuli
Sungud
Pitilian
Lanao Moros.
SEB.

Fig. 1.2. Lanao Moro Sultans Ambuli, Sungud, and Pitilian

so keen and heavy that with one blow they can almost cut the body of an adversary in two."[11]

Official fair literature also contributed heavily to notions of a volatile, savagely violent colonial subject. The souvenir guide to the Visayan Village, for example, spent an inordinate amount of space recounting the horrors that Visayan villagers endured from the "dreaded pirates of the southern seas" who terrorized the "helpless, panic-stricken people" for centuries. "For 300 long years," it explained, "the relentless and fanatical 'Sea Devils,' the Moros of Mindanao, continued to lay waste the Visayan villages, to rob the churches and homes, and to carry away into captivity the Visayan people. The spread of the Visayan population around the Mindanao and Sulu coasts is due almost entirely to the piracy of the Moros."[12] J. W. Buel, in his concomitant work on the fair, similarly warned fairgoers of this "fierce, cruel race" who "live almost entirely by piracy and robbery." Buel's most dire warnings, however, concerned the Moro tendency to transform into the dreaded "*juramentado.*"[13]

The term *juramentado* is Spanish for "oath taker." "Running juramentado" was a religious act of jihad against those who would threaten or pollute Islam. It was a specter that terrorized American colonists in the southern Philippines. Such suicide attackers typically engaged in elaborate rituals prior to their assaults, including ritualistic cleansing, shaving, body binding to prevent blood loss so as to prolong their attacks, donning symbolic clothing and magic amulets, the recitation of prayers, as well as polishing and sharpening weapons, which usually consisted of a kris and a barong. Once prepared the juramentado found a cluster of Christians and, shouting *"La ilaha il-la'l-lahu"* (There is no God but Allah), dispatched as many of the enemy as possible before meeting his desired martyr's death.[14] Although such acts terrified most Americans in the Philippines, there was also a strange sense of morbid delight surrounding the spontaneity, audacity, and religious mysticism of juramentados that pervaded colonial and mainstream American newspapers.[15] The *Mindanao Herald*, for example, printed sensational accounts of juramentado rituals:

> [In] the deserted forest, [with] the moonlight adding its rays to the weird and fantastic scene. At nightfall in the magic splendor of the moon, reverberates in the depth of the forest, warlike sounding metal like the everlasting lamenting echo of ever wandering souls, the priest congregates all the fame thirsting youths, [and] speaks of the strong ones who died a noble death in front of the enemy's steel . . . imagination crazes them; they convulsively grasp their krisses (sword) and imagine themselves feeling the cold sweat of death on their forehead. From the damp vapor of the night come voices installing valor into their hearts.[16]

Thus prepared, the Moro juramentado became the embodiment of fanatical determination, pushing the human body beyond limits scarcely conceived by most modern Americans. The fearlessness of their attacks and the unflinching endurance of pain inspired the popular American imagination and swelled a curiosity for the dreaded killers. Buel seized on the sensationalism of juramentado in his work, warning fair patrons: "When a Moro becomes tired of life, which is not unusual, he shaves off his eyebrows, puts on a white tunic, and presenting himself before a pantita, a pundit priest, he takes an oath to die killing Christians. His next step is to hide a kris or barong about his person and repairing to the nearest town cuts right and left everyone one he meets, whom he thinks is a Christian, until he is himself killed."[17]

Also related to the phenomenon of juramentado was a Malay concept known as running "amuck" or "amok." When a native "ran amuck" he, like the juramentado, engaged in crazed killing sprees, though unlike juramentados these massacres were indiscriminate and unaccompanied by religious preparations or fanaticism. Rather, they were explosive manifestations of pent-up frustration, shame, or depression acted out in violence and suicide. Hence, Filipinos, Moros, and even Americans theoretically had the potential to "run amok." Such acts of irrational violence were often attributed to weak mental conditions or the tropical heat, which made one's head "hot" and drove a person to insanity. Often, however, the concepts of juramentado and running amok were conflated in colonial reports as intertwined acts of a deranged mind, particularly associated with overly religious Moros.[18] In its "Descriptive Story of the Philippine Exhibit," the *World's Fair Bulletin* subtly warned readers not to buy too deeply into the "picturesque" image of romantic island life lest "some fanatical Moro takes it into his head to run 'Amok.'"[19]

If printed stories did not provide sufficient imagery, the material exhibits at the Moro Village presented constant prompts and corroborative affirmations of Moro violence. Krisses, kampilans, piras, barongs, and other edged weapons rested prominently next to a vast collection of spears and shields. Exhibit organizers also brought in twenty brass cannon, two outriggers, and a "large Moro pirate junk" to complete the bellicose display.[20] In the race for paid visitors, exhibit organizers strived to create a definitive narrative of savagery and violence. However, the real key to sensational marketing was to facilitate the illusion of proximate violence and observer participation. It was not enough to establish Moro cruelty and barbarism as an observable fact of Philippine life. Exhibit organizers had to bring the violence—or at least the threat of violence—out of the display and into the lives of the viewing public. Lewis, Wax, and their allies in the local press had to find a way to indulge the human urge to "tap on the glass," to provoke some kind of authentic, corroborative experience from the observed exhibits. At the St. Louis World's Fair in 1904, a new piece of technology provided the perfect opportunity.

Hunt, Capture, and Evade: Photography and Savagery

Following the introduction of George Eastman's Kodak No. 1 camera in 1888, Americans began a deep and abiding fascinating with amateur photography. For the first time in history, average Americans began producing visual re-creations of their lives and the lives of others. Through the mass production of images an emerging middle class could authenticate their experiences and create highly tailored visual narratives that both demonstrated and celebrated the fundamental uniqueness of their lives. Photography became a new form of biography. "Kodakers," as they came to be called, sought to capture images that told a story about their lives, to others and to themselves, affirming their relevance and subjectivity in an increasingly homogeneous world. Such ubiquitous image-making ultimately empowered middle-class Americans and democratized a new authority to speak on behalf of the world, independent of those who commanded an expertise in crafting empirically based historical narratives. In 1900 the cultural critic J. C. Abel offered a disdainful commentary on the phenomenon. This "phase of photography known as amateur," he wrote in *Modern Culture*, refers only to "the indiscriminate 'snap-shotting' of everything and everybody." These "kodackers are mere 'button pressers' . . . they cannot legitimately lay claim to being photographers. They have not even the right to say, 'Look at that picture. I did that!'" Although he acknowledged that cameras allowed regular Americans to "[create] for themselves permanent records of their travels and pleasures, of their friends, and of their foes," these images were ultimately unsanctioned and undisciplined by any knowledge of their contents.[21] Nevertheless, the trend rapidly expanded.

Photographs also offered a means to capture the life stories of others. In a burgeoning, consumer based, technology driven society, photographs became a sign of middle-class dominance and ownership. Those with the financial means could "capture" images of others, freeze them in space and time, and offer them up as corroborative evidence of the photographer's own experiences and personal narratives. Strange and exotic images were particularly effective in this regard. Shocking or sensual photographs of the exotic "other" verified the uniqueness of one's own experiences while simultaneously establishing one's vital credentials as a member of the powerful, white, middle-class establishment.[22]

The Louisiana Purchase Exposition offered an ideal opportunity to assert this sense of ownership and validation. "The Exposition is a paradise for kodakers," wrote one reporter for the *Daily Journal*.[23] In the course of a single day, camera-toting fairgoers could capture much of the world on their rolls of film. Encounters with exotic subjects could be preserved, revisited, and shown to others indefinitely.[24] These images represented not only an objectification of their contents but ownership as well—a kind of ownership that could never be shared or possessed by the photograph's subject, whose existential claim on that particular historical moment passed in an instant, to be retained only in the custody of another. Live exhibits were acutely aware of this asymmetrical claim to their visage and frequently resisted being photographed without consent or compensation. This presented kodakers with a thrilling pastime. Taking images of exotic or volatile "savages" became a precarious game of search, capture, and escape. Like colonial explorers treading frontier landscapes in exotic locales, kodakers at the World's Fair could search out native villages, native objects, and native bodies.[25] This adventure added reality to their simulated travel and provided a gripping backstory to their images. One fairgoer recalled capturing a photo of an unsuspecting Indian chief:

> I had carried the Kodak about all morning and not done much business, when on descending the steps from the government building I spied this old savage in all his glory. . . . "There's my game," said I. "I'll shoot him if I lose my scalp for it." I well knew the antipathy of the Indian to having his picture taken and that there was some danger attending the enterprise, but this was such a fine specimen I determined to take the chances. . . . I followed him a few paces and running quickly ahead, passed him and touched the button at the supreme moment. My next thought was to get away, for the old fellow had seen my camera and heard the shutter snap. . . . As he stopped in his tracks with a savage grunt I shot across the lawn. He stood there for a moment glaring at me and uttering grunts like a hog. . . . I headed for the Liberal Arts Building where I could lose myself in the crowd and render pursuit difficult. . . . But he resumed his path and I escaped with my prize.[26]

The vivid sense of a hunt, capture, danger, and escape in this account reveals a deep level of privileged engagement with live exhibits made possible by middle-class technologies. Although fair organizers did not officially promote or sanction this kind of illicit contact, the structure of the displays ultimately prompted fair patrons to engage in imperial behaviors and to indulge an imperial discourse of exoticism and savagery.

Both Wax and Lewis were quick to sensationalize the potential for danger at the Moro Village. Moros already enjoyed a robust reputation for volatility, violence, and religious fanaticism. Their supposed disdain for Americans had been spelled out in local newspapers prior to their arrival. To seize on this sensationalism fair organizers and managers created a veiled provocation in the form of a sober warning. "It is a violation of their Mohammedan faith for their photographs to be taken," advised an "Official Guide" to the fair, "and notices have been posted, notifying photographers of the danger of using cameras about this part of the reservation."[27] The *St. Louis Republic* and the *St. Louis Post-Dispatch* also ran extensive pieces cautioning the public against photographing the Moros—but always in a spirit of subtle provocation. "If you try to get a snap-shot or a photograph of the Moros at the World's Fair you'll do so at your own risk," taunted an article in the *St. Louis Republic*. In addition to "conspicuous" signs, guards were also "instructed to notify kodakers and camera fiends that they must not snap the Moros, and if they do it will be at their own risk, and if they got in trouble they must not blame the United States government in whose care the Moros are." The article is clear to equate "trouble" with violence. The "sign has been decided upon for fear [of] some photographer being boloed by an angry Moro. . . . You can't insult a Moro more than photographing him, and you're in luck if you're not chased off the reservation—and perhaps the earth—if you try the Kodak on him." Yet, amid all of these grave warnings, the columnist never explicitly forbids patrons from attempting a photograph, only notifying them that they are "taking a chance." The article then ends with a surprising invitation: "as some of the Moros get settled he'll welcome you if you leave the Kodak out." This parting line stands as an open invitation to flaunt photography equipment in front of the Moros. Even though it runs directly counter to the reporter's explanation of "the tenets of their religion . . . against images" and the deeply insulting nature of image capture, the article ultimately acknowledges the primacy of middle-class ownership and leaves it to the readers to answer the challenge.[28]

The *St. Louis Post-Dispatch* offered a similar provocation in an article entitled "Insure Your Life Before Photographing the Moros." However, rather than absolving the government of responsibility for potential violence, the *Post-Dispatch* excused the Moros, arguing that savagery was a known quantity and patrons should not be surprised by it. "Persons photographing the Moros do so at their own risk," warned the paper, "as [the Moros] are not responsible when they become enraged and would rather kill white people than not, it is considered dangerous to try to photograph them."[29] Again, fairgoers are not forbidden but only enticed with detailed descriptions of the risks involved in photographing colonial subjects.

With the game established, kodakers immediately took up the challenge, providing a spectacle of provocations that brought the display out of its constructed setting and into the lives of the viewers. In May 1904 the *St. Louis Post-Dispatch* recounted a violent encounter between a "camera fiend" and a Moro referred to as Rock-a-man. Despite Rock-a-man's "evident displeasure" at being photographed, the kodaker moved "up close [and] pointed the camera at the Moro." With "a yell of rage" Rock-a-man "leaped up, bolo in hand and started at the man with the camera." The photographer was so engrossed in his work that he did not realize what was happening. To his great fortune, "his friends, who were standing back a little way, admiring his nerve, shouted a warning." The kodaker turned with a start and "fled across the piles of bamboo, with the Moro in hot pursuit." When he reached his friends, the group formed a tight huddle and tried to dispose of the evidence. "The camera was concealed," recorded the paper, "and the Moro could not tell who was the man who tried to use it." Rock-a-man then "flourished his ugly-looking bolo and muttered imprecations." Other Moros soon joined in the altercation, "with their bolos in their hands," bearing down on the group of viewers. As circumstances became "threatening in the extreme," Charles Wax charged across the village "with all his speed, shouting in Arabic to Rock-a-man to withdraw." After much pleading and cajoling, the angry Moro finally "returned sulkily to his work, but his mood was so ugly that Mr. Wax took him to the Cuartel, where he would not be tempted again to use his bolo." This account demonstrated for mass audiences not only the exhilarating potential for violence at the Moro Village but a subtle admiration for those who would tread such dangerous ground. Like the photographer's friends, the paper saluted the man's courage, "admiring his nerve," and crafted the story as a commendation rather than a condemnation. There was a hunt, a capture, a deft use of wits to outsmart a "savage," and finally an escape enabled by colonial power. The encounter with Rock-a-man served as a short allegory for much of what the display represented. The thrilling adventures of a distant colonial periphery were brought home to America's heartland where average Americans could participate. The columnist ended his piece, not with a sober warning for other kodakers to exercise caution but with a solid reaffirmation of Moro volatility as a continued dare for those with the courage. "The Moros are dangerous fellows," he wrote, "who would rather kill a white man than eat."[30]

Despite the perilous nature of these accounts one must wonder to what degree such confrontations were actual performances on the part of the Moros. Although the newspapers sensationalized potential violence, no violence was ever actually inflicted on any fair patrons. It is very likely that in this simulated world of exoticism and adventure, the Moros acted out their proscribed roles to complete the carnival fantasy and attract visitors. As Bernard Cohn observed, "Everyone—rulers and ruled—had proper roles to play in the colonial sociological theater."[31] These roles came complete with costumes, cultural practices, and proscribed interactions. The Moro Village was marketed on certain expectations. The Moros were undoubtedly made aware of these expectations and likely knew how to capitalize on them.

"Savage" on "Savage" Violence

Violence against photographers was only part of a larger narrative concerning Moro volatility. Fair managers and the St. Louis press were quick to highlight any conflicts that might be sensationalized, including those with other live exhibits, fair officials, and particularly among the Moros themselves. In May 1904, for example, the *St. Louis Post-Dispatch* stoked a labor dispute between the Lanao Moros and Charles Wax. When contention arose concerning disbursement of salaries, the paper immediately ran a lengthy column reporting a "declared war upon W. H. Wax." The article described with carefully crafted language the Moros' "little Malay hearts [which] became . . . blazing coals [as they] panted for revenge." After holding a "war council," the aggrieved Moros "made up their minds to fight," the paper reported. "They did not know just what sort of fighting force Wax would send against them, but they would fight it [as] though it were the United States army." Despite this effusive buildup, the paper had to content it readers with only the imminent possibility of violence. In the end the two parties met through an intermediary to "effect a reconciliation," perhaps leaving observers disappointed, but still alert.[32]

Conflicts with other live exhibits were much more fruitful and entertaining. Moro enmity toward the US government was an effective way to circumscribe fairgoers within the realm of Moro violence, but watching the Moros battle other "savages" was a more comfortable form of entertainment.[33] Perhaps the most enduring spectacle of Moro on Moro violence took place in August 1904. In July of that year W. A. Long, a sergeant in the Twenty-Third Infantry, replaced Charles Wax as manager of the Lanao Moro Village.[34] Many prominent Moros took an immediate dislike to Long, whose "methods were different from those of his predecessor."[35]

Sultan Pitiilian, "ruler of 20,000," was foremost among his opponents. After the death of a high-ranking Moro, Sultan Pitiilian complained to Dr. W. P. Wilson, president of the Philippine Commission, and asked to have Long removed, as the death was deemed a bad omen. His request was denied. A bitter power struggle ensued between Pitiilian and Long, which eventually pitted the Moros against each other in a struggle for power. The dispute reached a head in mid-August when two Moros brandishing blades escaped from the village. After their capture Pitiilian openly denied Long's authority to discipline the runaways. For his insolence, the sultan was publicly deposed and stripped of his title by Frederick Lewis. In a ceremonial act of public humiliation the "big sign in front of [the sultan's] home proclaiming him ruler of 20,000 people was taken down." Immediately "there was a scramble among the [other] sultans for power." Tense factions formed, as Datus Mandal and Asume along with Sultans Songhalli and Sunbud sided with Long against Pitiilian and his allies Sultans Marahul, Lumbayaugui, and Ambulon. As tensions mounted so did anticipation for a violent showdown, which eventually occurred on August 22. Despite their antipathy, the feuding Moro were still required to attend to exhibition duties, including artistic reenactments of tribal violence in the form of dances and drama. In the midst of one such performance the participants suddenly "dropped their wooden swords and drew their daggers, slashing at one another viciously." The crowd erupted in cheers as "spectators thought they were getting an extra show for their money."

After several moments of intense combat the fight was halted. Two Moros sustained severe slashes across the head and were removed from the theater stage "badly wounded." Although the conflict suggested a "closely watched" potential for further violence, colonial discipline ultimately prevailed. A humbled Pitiilian soon "intimated his readiness to promise good behavior" if his title and privileges were returned.[36]

Hence, once again the Moro Village provided an unscripted allegory of savagery, violence, and the ultimate necessity for colonial power to protect and civilize. Through the lens of colonial exposition, fair patrons could quite literally witness the processes, methods, and rationales of imperial tutelage. The display sustained an overarching colonial discourse by selling empire to the American public as a form of reality entertainment. The circumstances and structures of the exhibit were carefully produced and meticulously explained, but its live exhibits, particularly in the case of the Moros, were often unscripted. This instability lent a sense of authenticity to the display. In the Moro Village, colonial authorities offered a window into the act of colonization rather than simply presenting an arrangement of trained colonial subjects. Yet this notion of instability was not easily maintained. The sensational aspects of the Moro Village had to extend beyond potential violence and into the realm of the freakish and disturbing.

Cannibalism

The St. Louis World's Fair has become well-known for its iconic innovations in popular food. Enterprising vendors pioneered a fusion of mobility, convenience, and taste to produce a radical shift in American consumption of fast food. In addition to viewing the various exhibits, fairgoers anticipated an array of culinary indulgences as they traversed the exposition grounds. At one time or another, the St. Louis World's Fair has been credited with the introduction of hotdogs, hamburgers, ice cream cones, cotton candy, peanut butter, iced tea, and the club sandwich, among many others. While these foods certainly existed prior to 1904, the St. Louis World's Fair instilled them deeply into America's collective consciousness.[37] The rise of popular "American" street foods also corresponded with a robust national conversation on sanitation, food processing, and public safety. Upton Sinclair's *The Jungle* brought this issue to the forefront of American discourse in 1906, only two years after the exposition.[38]

Among the most sensational and easily exploited characteristics of the "savage other" were their culinary habits. Fair patrons carried a certain expectation of oddity when viewing the live exhibits not only in appearance but also in habit. As Barbara Kirshenblatt-Gimblett explains: "The everyday lives of others are perceptible precisely because what they take for granted is not what we take for granted, and the more different we are from each other, the more intense the effect, for the exotic is the place where nothing is utterly ordinary. Such encounters force us . . . [to] pierce the membrane of our own quotidian world."[39] The daily consumption of food is perhaps the most quotidian and routine of all human habits. Yet eating has the uncanny power to entice or repulse with incredible effect. When establishing the sensational oddity of live exhibits fair managers were quick to point out that much of the display's "freakiness" had to do with eating.[40]

The St. Louis press, for example, obsessed for months over the "dog eating Igorrots" from the mountains of Luzon.[41] However, "as exposure exhausts novelty, new ways to raise the threshold of wonder must be found."[42] Charles Wax shrewdly realized that the intense competition for viewers at the Philippine Village would depend on his exhibit's ability to strike horror and wonder in the minds of fairgoers. If Igorrots received free press for eating dogs, Wax could easily go one better. In early May 1904 Charles Wax gave an interview to the *St. Louis Republic* in which he related a personal account of "the bloodiest and most awe-inspiring sight" anyone had ever seen in the Philippines. He stated that the Lanao Moros were "eaters of human flesh," "bloodthirsty cannibals," and the "most savage of the savages." He claimed to have witnessed an annual "barbaric feast of human flesh," in which slaves and prisoners, "fattened for the feast as we fatten cattle in the States for slaughter in the stock yards," were cast onto a pyramid of white-hot stones and roasted alive. After a sultan pronounced the offerings cooked, a crowd of one hundred thousand frenzied Moros tore the bodies apart with bamboo sticks as they feasted. Wax made sure to play his story to the extreme, proclaiming his subjects "the wildest and most savage people on the face of the globe today." "Human life counts for positively nothing among these Lanao Moros," he warned. "Murder is so common as to attract no attention."[43]

The story immediately circulated in newspapers across the country.[44] Soon Moro cannibalism became the prime motivator and rationale for Moro savagery. The Moros' supposed lusty celebration of dead American troops, for example, was explained within the context of a dark desire for human flesh. "Cannibal appetites were whetted yesterday morning at the Philippine reservation at the news of the . . . slaughtering of American soldiers by Moros," reported the *St. Louis Republic*. Amid their "great rejoicings" the Moros made a formal "request for a slave to kill and serve up" at a celebratory feast. The Philippine Commission reportedly refused their request. "Although, it is the custom to eat a slave at any festivity of the kind, they were told that they would have to get along on chicken and rice," explained the paper.[45]

Wax made every effort to exploit and perpetuate the horrors of cannibalism for the duration of the fair. He cast dreadful rumors in anticipation of an upcoming cannibal feast in early October 1904, not coincidentally to coincide with the fair's conclusion. The *St. Louis Republic* informed its readers that Mr. Wax was yet "planning what he will do when October 7 comes around and his barbarians demand their annual human-blood meal. Of all the savages in the Philippines these Lanao Moros are the most vicious and bloodthirsty. They require watching every minute of the day and great care is exercised to see that visitors are properly warned of their danger when around them." Wax was careful to maintain a tenuous position of assuring the public of his authority and control, while simultaneously suggesting the constant possibility of violent savage outbursts. "The human offering has been handed down since the beginning of time," Wax explained, "it positively cannot be prohibited. . . . [I]t is utterly out of the question for the army to prohibit them." Nevertheless, Wax encouraged the fair patrons not to worry: "I am carefully guarding the public against them so that I don't believed there is any danger, but as the most savage of the savages of the world, they are naturally a curiosity."[46]

These tales of Moro cannibalism were almost certainly a publicity stunt contrived specifically to bolster attendance at the Moro exhibit. There is no documented evidence of cannibalism in the southern Philippines to be found in any official colonial record. Commission reports, censuses, ethnographic accounts, and local news publications are conspicuously devoid of any references to Moro cannibalism. Yet these stories at the St. Louis World's Fair went unchallenged by both Filipino participants and colonial authorities. Like the Igorrot's exotic culinary habits, Moro consumption of human flesh was seemingly acknowledged as part of an acceptable theatrical dimension to the exposition, where "it became difficult, if not impossible, to distinguish between what was real, what was simulated, and what was total fantasy."[47]

The "savage" exhibits were not meant to provide a strict museological display of artifacts. There was very little value in the bare exhibition of acquired items, including human beings. The exhibits as a whole were meant to teach more fundamental lessons demonstrating high truths about the nature of the world and the necessity of empire. As Spencer Crew and James Sims observe: "Authenticity [in exhibitions] is not about factuality or reality. It is about authority."[48] Wax and other fair organizers were marketing ideas and narratives more than they were marketing objects. The "truth" or "falsity" of the Moro exhibit was more a matter of maintaining a particularly "truthful" narrative than presenting empirically established facts. The public needed educating. Theatrical methods were an acceptable pedagogical tactic, which also had the added advantage of padding the finances of those engaged in such pedagogies. Yet, despite the overarching pedagogical aims of exposition authorities, the Moro exhibit simultaneously provoked a number of counter discourses. Americans of all stations began to see self-reflexive images and familiar messages in the muddled and dynamic contours of the Moro display. Market forces determined by public demand did not solely seek out the strange and exotic. Fairgoers, and even fair organizers, frequently sought out and crafted recognizable and comforting themes in unexpected places. While the Moro Village could serve as a window to exotic landscapes in a savage and unfamiliar colonial frontier, the exhibit could also provide a polished mirror that revealed and revived cherished elements of a fading American past.

NOSTALGIA AND THE FAMILIAR SAVAGE

As fair patrons approached the Philippine exhibit they passed by an unmistakable landmark situated prominently in front of the Agricultural Palace. Engineers and horticulturists had collaborated to create the world's largest clock, measuring one hundred feet in diameter and studded with over thirteen thousand flowers. While its immense size and grandeur were remarkable, the clock's true genius was in its precision. A vast collection of gears, wheels, springs, and pinions assembled in a shaft beneath the clock face measured time in thousandths of a second.[1]

This astonishing mechanism stood as a monument to modern time; an unyielding, quantifiable, mechanical measure of humankind's march into the future. The clock also represented an acute awareness of temporality, which permeated virtually every corner of the exposition. The St. Louis World's Fair was designed to stand as a testament to modernity. However, modernity could only be demonstrated and ultimately affirmed through relative comparison. Therefore, the exposition required a variety of "times"—some lesser and some greater—to demonstrate the triumph of the present and the inevitability of a particular future. As the owner of *Cosmopolitan Magazine*, John Brisben Walker, stated in his feature article on the fair: "Expositions accentuate the deficiencies of the past, give us a realization of our present advantages, [and] predict the development of the near future."[2] J. W. Buel further expounded upon this concept of multiple temporalities existing within a simultaneous historical moment: "the periods which, for facility of classification, we designate as the Paleolithic, Neolithic, bronze, and iron ages do not in fact mark successive stages of the world's progress, but rather indicate the advances of particular peoples, since the stone age of one country may be contemporaneous with the iron, or electrical age of another."[3]

This relative temporal existence was precisely what the fair was designed to demonstrate. It was meant to serve as a conclusive affirmation of the superiority of American industrial modernity, borne out through a collage of empirical evidence scientifically assembled and exhibited before the world. Despite the incessant drumbeat of progress, however, the fair both revealed and catered to an overwhelming sense of nostalgia. While the technological world of tomorrow could inspire awe and wonder, it also enhanced smoldering anxieties as known and cherished pasts faded from existence. These modern anxieties have been well documented in the works of T. J. Jackson Lears, Richard Wightman Fox, Peter Fritzsche, Goran Blix, Zygmunt Bauman, and Richard Hofstadter, among others.[4] Frederick Jackson Turner similarly articulated these concerns more than a decade prior to the fair in his famous "frontier thesis" delivered at the 1893 Chicago World's Fair.[5]

As primarily middle-class Americans gazed into an increasingly homogenized, banal, and tediously mechanized future it sparked a crisis of conservation. There was a cultural scramble to recover, preserve, and experience treasured elements from the past. Foremost among these elements was the concept of masculinity. Gail Bederman, Kristin Hoganson, J. A. Mangan, James Walvin, and many others have carefully documented the United States' dramatic nineteenth-century shift away from "manliness" and toward "masculinity."[6] The old manly values of gentility, forbearance, civility, and moderation gave way in the nineteenth-century to new masculine standards of forceful violence and virulent sexuality, standards that played themselves out in dramatic ways on the American frontier.[7] As the American western wilderness increasingly fell under the ubiquitous and regulating gaze of industrial modernity, many Americans worried how these new masculine values would be taught and demonstrated without a frontier. It is worth recalling Theodore Roosevelt's dedicatory speech to the exposition in which he nostalgically praised "the old days" and the "mighty qualities" of "courage and resolution . . . tenacity and fertility." He closed with the ambivalent charge that "we must insist upon [these] strong, virile virtues," while simultaneously observing the peaceful values of modern civil society.[8]

This dilemma of reconciling the old and the new required a fresh frontier. "American values" could be reproduced and perpetuated on distant colonial peripheries where dramatic manifestations of sex and violence mediated the inevitable overcivilizing and emasculating effects of industrial modernity.[9]

Most Americans, however, would never experience these colonial frontiers. Instead, traditional values had to be inscribed through observation and vicarious participation. In 1904 the preeminent child psychologist G. Stanley Hall argued forcefully that exposure to savagery was essential to the healthy development of young men. In addition to serving as president of both the American Psychological Association and Clark University, Hall pioneered psychological theories of race making during adolescence. He was particularly concerned with the emasculating effects of modernity on young boys. Consequently, Hall advocated maintaining a Darwinistic struggle for racial supremacy by exposing young men to savagery, thus honing their competitive skills. By maintaining a visceral connection with primitive man (known as racial recapitulation), Hall believed that young American men would not lose their competitive edge and succumb to racial suicide.[10] The Louisiana Purchase Exposition served as an excellent opportunity for such exposure, not only for young men but for all fairgoers.

A New Frontier

The Moro Village was especially well suited for these therapeutic and pedagogical aims. The southern Philippines functioned as the distant frontier of a distant colonial frontier. Its wild, untamed land and "savage" populations had become hallmarks of American exotic fantasies of the

Philippines. In the years leading up the exposition, the American public was titillated by fantastic stories of Moro savagery and frontier violence. These stories were always firmly situated within the familiar trope of an American western frontier. In 1899, for example, John F. Bass of *Harper's Weekly* published an extensive article on the frontier nature of Moros. "Like a western mining-camp of old," he analogized, "[the southern Philippines] is full of adventure . . . [where] a native is quick to draw his knife, just as an American desperado was to draw his revolver." The remarkable similarities between far-off Moro Province and the American West were ultimately explained by the Moros' "manliness and independence of character," a requisite of frontier life "not found among the Indians in the rest of the Philippines."[11]

Official government reports were no less romantic in their indulgence of dime novel fantasies in Moro Province. The colonial census of 1903 suggested that the southern Philippines was a violent frontier where "every [Moro] when outside of his house or away from home is armed either with a kris or barong, the two weapons of warfare."[12] Perhaps the most explicit equivalence between frontier Americans and Moros came from Colonel John Roberts, who worked extensively throughout Moro Province in the years prior to the exposition. He recalled, "Just as the American of the Western Frontier in the nineteenth century expressed the quintessence of the Anglo-Saxon racial characteristics—individuality, adventurousness, and the desire to build from fresh material—so the Moro was the Malay frontiersman of the Far East; in him the Malay traits blossomed into a virile race."[13] Virility, masculinity, courage, adventure, and individuality were all qualities that Americans not only recognized but desperately sought to preserve in a world of relentless modernization.[14]

These preexisting tropes naturally worked their way into press accounts and exposition literature. Alongside shocking descriptions of Moro degeneracy and savagery, fairgoers could also find a seemingly paradoxical abundance of admirable profiles, highlighting the Moros' noble frontier masculinity and grit. These two discourses resided side by side in a kind of strange symbiosis—horrible shocking tales brought curious patrons in while familiar frontier tropes endeared the exhibits to nostalgic observers. The southern Philippines "is without any population to speak of; it has no ancient customs to live down," boasted a *Souvenir of the Philippine Exposition.* "There is practically 25,000,000 acres of virgin forest and agricultural land . . . as free as the air."[15] Like the American West, this land produced "courageous savages" and preserved them "by deadly climate and barriers of mountains, marshes and impenetrable brakes."[16] In so many ways, American observers were looking for and looking at popular romantic images of their "primitive selves" in the Moro Village.[17] This process of self-rediscovery was not only a key component of the Moro Village, but the exposition at large. In their respective works, Jon Zachman and Martha Clevenger have highlighted the "insatiable" and "immediate" demands for nostalgia at the World's Fair.[18]

This yearning on the part of American fair patrons becomes even clearer when informed by the work of Johannes Fabian. In his book *Time and the Other*, Fabian analyzes the critical temporal function of ethnography as a means of capturing an autobiographical past through the formation of an objectified "other." Like Lears, Fabian explores the therapeutic value of a controlled retreat into a recognizable past. He argues that what "makes the savage significant to the evolutionist's Time is that he lives in another Time." This enables the ethnographer—and those consuming his or her work—to experience a multiplicity of temporalities at their leisure; allowing for the technological convenience and ethnopolitical power of the present as well as the supposed simplicity and quietude of the preindustrial past. In each case, "directly or vicariously, anthropological discourse formulates knowledge that is rooted in an author's autobiography."[19] In other words, whether in the past or the present, ethnographic display both communicates and affirms narratives relating to the ethnographer rather than to the object of study.

This was certainly manifested in the ambivalent and seemingly paradoxical discourses characterizing the Louisiana Purchase Exposition. Both the Philippine and the Moro Villages were designed and constructed to demonstrate the "deficiencies of the past," which was marked by savagery.[20] This stark comparison provided a pedagogical context meant to guide patrons toward affirmative conclusions regarding American state and industrial power. Yet, despite these aims, fairgoers brought their own deeply ambivalent feelings about modernity, which they channeled into unexpected demands for nostalgic indulgence. The market-oriented nature of the displays naturally accommodated this demand, drawing familiar parallels and indulging the autobiographic functions of ethnography. In this way American observers were able to effect an organic reappropriation of broadly intended exposition messages at the Moro Village. With the aid of the press and even fair literature, Americans of all stations subtly projected themselves onto the displays in ways that affirmed and celebrated a fading past rather than a burgeoning industrial present. As Fabian observes: "The posited authenticity of a past (savage, tribal, peasant) serves to denounce an inauthentic present (the uprooted, *évolués*, acculturated)."[21] The world of modern industrial wonders was also a world of anonymity, artificiality, cold mechanization, and disenchanting science. The past held a certain authenticity. It was known. It was understood. And in this sense it provided a safe retreat, even if only in the form of entertainment.

Familiar Subjects

The Moros embodied at least two broad characteristics that served to define them as familiar historic subjects to nostalgic Americans. First, the Moros were seen as industrious, with a particular disposition toward innovation and the acquisition of wealth. Although many Americans had doubts regarding the uncertainties of industrial modernity, the historical path to its achievement was revered.[22] It was the journey rather than the destination that came to define romantic images of American exceptionalism. Work, grit, innovation, frugality, and perseverance were all qualities demanded by the frontier, which translated into a unique American experience. As a writer for the *Mindanao Herald* observed: The American frontier "has been the magic caldron into which has been poured a great stream of immigration . . . [and] out of which has come in the second generation Americans bearing the mind and stamp of American character."[23]

The United States had now acquired a new frontier, and with it a new race of rising entrepreneurs, which, inherently incentivized by the prospects of wealth and industry, could recapitulate a cherished chapter in American history. Much of the primary literature concerning the Moro Village makes emphatic mention of the Moros' deep and healthy respect for material wealth. This quality marked a sharp departure from other "savage" groups who were supposedly content in their primitive poverty. "As a general rule," remarked a souvenir guide, "the [Moro] men are industrious and there are to be found among them carpenters, blacksmiths, silversmiths, bricklayers, tailors and even gunsmiths of fair ability."[24] The *St. Louis Post-Dispatch* agreed: "[The Moros] are the dudes of the Philippines. . . . The Moros are great market traders and the market is the chief institution in every Moro Village. Moro children are a sturdy lot, their grand health and strength being due to the outdoor life they live. . . . Some of the Moros are quite advanced."[25] Among these "advanced" Moros was Rajah Muda Mandi of Zamboanga, whom the *Official Guide, Louisiana Purchase Exposition* praised as a well-traveled cosmopolitan, wealthy "by American standards," and well acquainted with the "luxuries and conveniences of Western Civilization."[26] Datu Facundo received similar admiration from the *St. Louis Post-Dispatch*. The paper commended the tribal leader for his discerning taste and dignified demeanor. The Moros "are the 'swell' dressers of the Philippines," explained one article. "Datto Facundo, their chief, is the Berry Wall of Zamboanga. All the men of the tribe are dudes and they come as near to the sartorial perfection of the chief as they can without being guilty of *lese majeste*. The toilettes of the women are just as brilliant. . . . The women who go to see the Moro women in their lake houses on Arrowhead will rave over the garments of their eastern sisters."[27]

An awareness of material fashion and concerns for competitive consumption made the Moros immediately relatable to American patrons. The *St. Louis Post-Dispatch*, for example, ran stories placing Moros at the very center of the irresistible hurricane of commercialism inundating the fair. In September 1904 the paper described a fashion craze for gold teeth among the Samal Laut. "A gold teeth fad has broken out in the Moro Village," declared a reporter. After being lured into a downtown "tooth emporium" by a "spieler," one of the Samal Moros paid to replace a tooth lost in battle with a gold replica. "The Moros think a great deal of their teeth," explained the author of the article, so "when he went back to the village he was so proud that he wouldn't speak to the other Moros." When his countrymen "discovered what had so greatly enlarged his pride . . . they were filled with envy [and] set up a clamor for gold teeth." Their requests were so fervent that "to avert an uprising, [manager Lewis] agreed that all who had room for them might buy gold teeth." Even those with strong incisors, concluded the columnist, "will not be satisfied until they have front teeth extracted to make room for the gold ones."[28]

While this story certainly indulged in a kind of lighthearted observation of perceived Moro naiveté and childlike wonder for shiny things, the Moros' experience with the tooth emporium was not exclusive to "primitives." Burton Benedict points out that one of the primary underlying purposes of the World's Fair was to foster and indulge "the new middle class" with an emphasis on "techniques of production" and "the latest patterns of consumption."[29] Jon Zachman and James Gilbert similarly argue that American fair patrons were commercial pilgrims, searching out material items and souvenirs to "preserve" and "validate the authenticity" of their experience.[30] Like the Moros, wide-eyed American fairgoers were similarly lured into shops and roadside stands by clever spielers where they were seduced into buying commemorative plates, cups, coins, stamps, buttons, spoons, figurines, and all manner of trinkets, as well as the latest fashions. Hence, while the media may have indulged in subtle mockery of the Moros' enchantment with the Tooth Emporium, it also spoke of a deeply shared experience for both colonizer and colonized at the fair. Commercialism and competitive consumption ensnared native exhibit and American patron alike. The unplanned dimensions of the exposition did not discriminate based on race or political status. In this way there was something significantly familiar about the Moros; something Americans could recognize and appreciate in their fellow travelers at the fair.

A flurry of articles over the summer enhanced this notion by extolling the Moros' inherently innovative and industrious spirit. Not only did Moros have a natural and healthy desire for material progress, they also fundamentally understood the work and genius required to obtain modern comforts. An article in the *St. Louis Post-Dispatch* in early May 1904 marveled at the Moros' work ethic upon arriving at the fairgrounds. The paper reported that the Moros "were too busy to eat. They preferred to work rather than eat. They are the first people to turn deaf ears to the dinner bell on the World's Fair grounds. They passed up chow because they were at work on their village and they are so anxious to get into Moro houses that they did not want to lose the time it would take to go to the cuartel and get their dinner."[31] This piece and others like it affirmed a strong preexisting consensus among military leaders and colonial authorities concerning Moro industriousness. In the years leading up to the fair, government ethnographic accounts commented heavily upon the Moros' propensity for industry and labor. The colonial census of 1903 was particularly explicit. Colonial authorities praised the Moros, who were "known to do very hard work" despite being "victims of environment . . . where the climate offers but little encouragement to either energy or ambition."[32] Their exceptional work ethic established a natural protoindustrial framework where Moros inherently recognized "the necessity for trades and craftsmen in even the small division of labor which their social organization affords."[33] The *Mindanao Herald* similarly observed this protocapitalist predisposition, pointing out that the Moros already had commercial and service specialists who were viably "industrious" prior to American inducement.[34]

This established work ethic and desire for material gain was a cause for great celebration among Americans eager to see the effects of tutelary colonialism. While education and democratic institutions had their place, hard work was ultimately the key to industrial modernity and civil society. A writer in the *Mindanao Herald* summed up the principle: "The Filipinos can never become a strong, robust, self-reliant people without working as we have worked, and without that training which comes with work . . . work—which has made the Aryan people the arbiters of the destiny of the world. . . . Work, hard work, is necessary to the higher development of all physical, mental, and moral life."[35] Another editorial similarly concluded, "There is but one way to reclaim this unfortunate country [the Philippines], and that is through the medium of material prosperity, which after all, is the only civilizer."[36]

Such principles were not solely the tools of colonial instruction, however, for most Americans considered work a universal principle of progress, objectively applicable to all. "Crime everywhere [is] decreased [with] less drunkenness and less tendency to crime," trumpeted an article in Manila's *Daily Bulletin* praising the uplifting power of work. The prospects for acquiring material wealth brought "with it a feeling of hope that it is now easier to earn a living than to steal it."[37] The Moros were particularly exceptional in this regard, as early colonial tropes characterized Christian Filipinos as hopelessly indolent, lacking motivation and failing to understand the principles of progress.[38] Alternatively, Moros provided a bright spot of hope for American tutelary objectives in the Philippines. More than this, they again presented Americans with something intimately recognizable, something nostalgic. Moros seemed to harbor qualities that

Americans saw in themselves and would like to revive in a new age of mechanized modernity.

Press coverage on this subject at the fair tended to focus more on Moro children. There was a deep infatuation with the young Moros' innate intelligence and natural desires to innovate, to build, and to save money. In July 1904 the *St. Louis Post-Dispatch* ran a feature article on an exceptional young Moro boy named Dowina. According to the report, Dowina delighted in doing "double work," attending both the Christian Visayan and "wild" peoples' school sessions. Dowina enjoyed "special privileges" because of his exceptional diligence and was allowed to wear "the turban of his countrymen" among the Christian children. The reporter was especially impressed with the "uncivilized" students and "wondered that there was no misbehavior on the part of the little wild children." The paper observed:

> No one attempted to throw a paper ball. No one whispered and those that weren't reciting were saying the sounds over to themselves. Nobody broke school rules. . . . They didn't laugh at each other when mistakes were made, but everyone tried as hard as possible to say things as their teacher did. . . . When the session was done Miss Zamora unlocked the door. The wildest of the children stood up, but she told them to sit down and they did.[39]

This diligence toward education bespoke familiar desires to an emerging American middle class, which similarly viewed education as the key to social and financial mobility. The young Moros' conscientious approach to their studies reflected the hopes of thousands of fair visitors for their own children and, in a brief moment, flipped the script of colonial display by positing Dowina as an object lesson for Americans rather than an imperial subject in need of civilizing.

The local press was also quick to link Moro children's vigor for education with an acute desire for wealth. This association was thought to manifest an explicitly modern understanding of the machinations underlying mobility and success.[40] The *St. Louis Post-Dispatch*, for example, heralded the story of a seven-year-old Moro boy named Leoc. The young man was described as "one of the diminutive Filipinos who dived for pennies in Arrowhead Lake." Yet, despite his low status and meager vocation, Leoc had a burning "ambition to be rich." With stalwart determination,

Leoc "begged every visitor . . . to test his diving abilities. Never a penny has been flipped over the waters of Arrowhead Lake without an accompanying splash and Leoc disappear[ing] after it." Day after day the young Moro secretly stashed his coins in a bamboo tree. In late October 1904 Manager Lewis discovered the cache and retrieved $127 worth of pennies, nickels, and dimes. Lewis promptly turned the entire amount over to Leoc without reservation. When asked what he would do with such a sizable amount of money the young boy responded that he would like to "take it home and someday go into the insurrection business."[41] While such bold anti-imperial sentiments from a young colonial subject might have normally provoked alarm, the paper passed it off with a subtle nod of admiration. Leoc earned his money through hard work and was therefore entitled to spend it as he wished. The article punctuated the point with a large photo of Leoc dressed in a button-down Moro coat and fez with tassels hanging playfully just above his brow. The young man bore a broad, tooth-filled smile of accomplishment. Like Dowina's achievements through education, Leoc's saving represented the desires of virtually every American visitor for themselves or their children. Such stories from the Moro Village affirmed Americans' notion of the United States as a land of opportunity, even for those without the advantages of privileged birth. Leoc's ability to save the equivalent of nearly two months' salary for the average American machinist at the time by diving for tourist coins at the meager age of seven bespoke endless possibilities and fueled middle-class dreams that fair organizers sought to instill.[42]

Young Moros perhaps found their greatest compatibility with the underlying messages of the fair by demonstrating a drive for innovation. President Francis declared the exposition "a true and complete festival of progress," demonstrated primarily through displays of "man's handiwork" and innovation.[43] The Board of Directors' plans similarly called for a specific focus on "inventive genius" as a defining characteristic of the fair's overall approach.[44] As early as March 1904, American newspapers began to take a keen interest in the inherent innovative impulses among Moro youth. An article in the *Chicago Daily Tribune*, for example, remarked upon the dramatic changes to youthful recreation in the United States at the turn of the century. The mechanized nature of industrial modernity inspired young minds to craft a variety of devices and toys from common household items. Diagrams of homemade roller skates, musical instruments, and works of art splashed across the news page with American youngsters in various attitudes of recreation. "But," proclaimed the article, "of all Uncle Sam's younger generation the little brown Moro lads of the Philippines are most resourceful in creating amusing toys when their opportunities are taken into consideration." The paper provided a sketch of two Moro boys quietly contemplating a homemade bamboo cart with spool wheels and a top made of nipa palm leaves. Unlike the American children dashing about in carefree play, the Moro youths are depicted in thoughtful poses, with their arms folded, chins tucked, and eyes fixed in profound contemplation. They look like older, wiser men in young boys' bodies. The marvel of their creation was made all the more profound by their "primitive" circumstances. Unlike American children, the Moros were bereft of inspiring models and cutting edge technologies to foster new ideas. Their innovative impulses were purely organic. This was cause for celebration as Moro children represented latent industrialists, lacking only the technologies of modernity to bring their designs to fruition. The Moros' propensity for imitation and progress was further confirmed when US soldiers began to introduce American activities in Moro Province. "In less than a week" after introducing tennis, "the Moro lads were at it in good form," reported the *Chicago Daily Tribune* in March 1904. The boys astutely made "rackets . . . with bamboo handles and catgut strings . . . fixed to a piece of hooped wood." They also constructed serviceable balls from "split bamboo, platted and filled out."[45] This was more than mere imitative instinct, however. The Moro youths were not simply aping American behavior. They were taking "American" ideas and furnishing them with innovative technological solutions constructed from available materials unique to their own environment. Such impulses seemed to represent the essence of American theories of economic development in the colonial Philippines and fueled aspirations for successful colonial tutelage in Moro Province.

The local St. Louis Press was similarly fascinated with the young Moros' remarkable inclination toward innovation. In August 1904 the *St. Louis Post-Dispatch* published a series of articles documenting the construction of a "shoot-the-chutes" in Moro Village. While walking along the pike two Moro boys, named Lao and Fasuda, observed fairgoers racing down a log flume ride know as a "shoot-the-chutes," and "it made a quick hit" with the youths. Upon returning to their village the young

Fig. 2.1. Moro boys riding a "shoot the chutes" they built on Arrowhead Lake

Fig. 2.2. Moro children diving in Arrowhead Lake

men set about constructing a steeply inclined bamboo flume "between thirty and forty feet long." After greasing it with soap, the boys "carried their little dugout canoe onto the bridge, laid it on the incline, climbed in and zip! Splash! They had a shoot-the-chutes" all their own. The speed with which these perceptive young Moros "picked up this adjunct of civilization" and adapted themselves to the "world of fun" available in the United States left a lasting impression on observers. It also portended positive developments in Moro Province. While the head of the Moro Village, Datto Facundo, distanced himself from the shoot-the-chutes, forbidding his warriors to participate in activities "beneath the dignity of a grown man," the youths had no such cultural compunctions. Their early exposure to American culture and technology promised to shatter archaic cultural impulses and open the way for a prosperous industrial future. Despite objections from the older generation, "the chutes will be among the innovations introduced in Morodom this winter [upon their return to the Philippines]," predicted one reporter.[46]

Many Americans seemed particularly concerned that the Moro children's potential not be wasted. By the end of the fair in November 1904, the War Department, in concert with private interests and the St. Louis press, began prompting socially conscious Americans to adopt Moro children. The *St. Louis Post-Dispatch*, for example, ran the story of Mrs. Charles Wentz of Baltimore who fell in love with a ten-year-old Moro girl named Tabac and determined to adopt the child. Mrs. Wentz relentlessly petitioned the War Department with letters and requests until at last the adoption was granted. Tabac's story served as an invitation to all like-minded American families who might want to contribute to the civilizing mission. "If other American families want Filipino children," the paper reported, "they have only to convince Secretary of War Taft and Chairman Lawshe of the Philippine commission of their reliability." However, interested parties "will be expected to take the little Filipinos into their homes and teach them American ways. They must be sent to school, educated into American clothes, as well as language and pursuits." Through these charitable efforts, "the War Department has a faint hope that these and other adoptions may help in the task of benevolent assimilation."[47]

While the end of the article stood as an open invitation to adopt Filipinos generally, the author appealed to readers by sharing the story of a Moro child whose burgeoning potential had been established and promoted throughout the course of the fair. Unlike Christian Filipinos, thought to be corrupted, emasculated, and damaged by Spanish parochialism, Moros represented a more pristine colonial subject. This notion inspired Americans eager to apply the humanistic-minded objectives of American imperial tutelage.[48] While Moro proclivity toward innovation and material wealth suggested a potentially shared historical trajectory with Americans, fairgoers were also tantalized by the more taboo aspects of savagery. Modern civilization brought a privileged sense of cultural and ethnic superiority to many Americans, but it also came at the cost of forbearance. Self-consciously progressive citizens emphatically renounced certain archaic social and sexual practices deemed nonconducive to civil society. Such renunciations served to establish one's credentials as a member of the civilized elite and validated moral disdain of the savage "other." This morally rigid façade frequently gave way to vicarious forms of taboo behavior, however. Just as twenty-first-century Americans patronize forms of media that depict and celebrate violent or sexual fantasies, fairgoers were also eager to participate in vicarious forms of taboo indulgence.

Sanitizing the Taboo through Exhibition

Part of the allure of Moro culture was its unabashed acceptance of behaviors and practices once found in American history but now considered morally reprehensible. Although a majority of fairgoers likely did not agree with institutions such as slavery and polygamy, voyeuristic participation in such practices offered a kind of acceptable nostalgic indulgence. Slavery, for example, had tremendous appeal for curious patrons. In her work "Headhunter Itineraries," Vernadette Vicuna Gonzalez demonstrates how the "visual tropes of empire" were not limited exclusively to imperial projects abroad but were also rooted firmly within "the space of the U.S. South, which was hospitable to such racial taxonomies." In a region of rapidly changing social dynamics, many fairgoers sought out "comforting templates for the unsettled racial narrative of the postbellum South."[49] One such template took the form of "The Old Plantation." Heralded as a "reminder of the ante-bellum days in Dixie," twentieth-century Americans could observe "the picturesque darky of ante-bellum days," including "colored mammies," "pickaninnies," buck and wing dancing, minstrels shows, and "negro cabins."[50] These kinds of quaint displays effectively "homogenized and sanitized the pre–Civil War years in the American South" and allowed for tolerable appreciation of an inhuman practice.[51]

Many Americans demonstrated a similar fascination and appreciation of Moro slavery. Although there was an initial outpouring of moral indignation over forced servitude in Moro Province, by 1899 colonial officials and many news outlets began to reassess the sinister nature of slavery as practiced in the southern Philippines.[52] An article in *Harper's Weekly* in 1899, for example, argued that "slavery in the Sulus is by no means the dreadful thing that the word suggests."[53] The 1901 Philippine Commission Report agreed, pointing out that in "the majority of cases slaves are treated kindly" and incorporated into their master's family. Moreover, "military officers everywhere expressed the opinion that Moro slaves were, on the whole, so well satisfied with their lot that if they were all set free, the majority of them would promptly return to their old masters and voluntarily take up their old life again."[54] The census of 1903 also confirmed that Moro slavery was "almost nominal" and that "many bond servants prefer the secure and easy life they lead in the household of a stronger master."[55] By 1904 colonial newspapers were asserting that slavery in Moro Province was not only a tolerable form of social patronage but an important step in the Moros' historical progress. "Slavery is not merely an institution it is also a stage in evolution," read an ethnographic account in the *Mindanao Herald*, "and many of the slaves of this region are yet at the low stage of development at which the mild slavery in which they live suits them better than freedom."[56]

These softer assessments were remarkably similar to arguments made by slavery apologists in the antebellum South. In 1863, for example, H. T. Utley foreshadowed the *Mindanao Herald*'s assessment when he argued, "According to history, the institution of slavery was universally made almost an indispensable incident to the organization and maintenance of civilized government, for it was an institution anterior to government itself." For all great civilizations, "slavery was an indispensable element."[57]

Hence, though most Americans in 1904 vehemently opposed slavery in principle, there was perhaps a measure of recognition of its supposed historical value as a phase in human evolution. This sense of relative historicism allowed a certain tolerance for Moro slavery as an antiquated custom practiced by premodern people, who were themselves engaged in their own process of lagging evolution. Assessments of Moro slavery also echoed antebellum religious justifications for the practice. Apologists such as R. W. Warren, H. T. Utley, T. W. Hoit, C. Blancher Thompson, Thornton Stringfellow, and others argued that slavery was an essential and honored institution among the "chosen" children of Abraham, and that the great patriarch himself kept slaves "by infallible law of the Almighty," thus "establishing, upholding, and justifying slavery among the Jewish nation."[58] In 1902. Military Governor of the Philippines Arthur MacArthur similarly categorized Moro slavery as an Abrahamic and religiously motivated institution. "The Moros are a Mohammedan people," he explained to a Senate committee, "they are a patriarchal people. They live in these relations [of servitude], as I said before, and it is most unfortunate that the English word 'slave' is ever used there, because it is very misleading in its meaning."[59] Hence, much like the Old Plantation, Moro slavery had been effectively contextualized and sanitized by 1904, making it socially and politically acceptable as a medium of entertainment at the World's Fair.[60]

In early May 1904 the *St. Louis Post-Dispatch* ran an extensive profile on Moro slavery at the exposition. "Many visitors to the World's Fair will for the first time see human beings held in slavery," the paper teased. Lest readers doubt the veracity of the exhibit, the article gave detailed statements regarding the literal nature of the institution.

> When a sultan runs out of retainers he goes to war with a neighboring sultan, and if he wins he comes back with a long train of human loot. If he loses . . . he is compelled to make his own living until he can get together a new crop of slaves. Formerly these slaves were bought and sold, but when the United States took possession of the islands a proclamation was issued prohibiting the traffic in human flesh, which has recently been accepted by the sultans, who now can obtain new chattels only by conquest.

Yet despite this horrific description of trafficked human beings, the *St. Louis Post-Dispatch* was careful to place the practice within a sanitized narrative of contextual evolution. "There are a hundred of the slaves," the paper continued, "and they appear to take their bondage in a matter-of-fact way.

If they chafe under their restraint they show no evidence of it." Even exposure to the vast freedoms of the United States did not seem to alter their
culturally programmed subservience. "It may be asked why these slaves
from the Orient do not seek to be free now that they are in the land that
plays freedom in the headlines. . . . It is likely . . . that the vastness of this
country, as well as its customs and language, to which they are all unac-
customed, would deter them from running away, even if they had the
opportunity to do so."[61] Hence, fairgoers were not witnessing a human
atrocity per se but, rather, a relic institution practiced by premodern people. This relative historical or evolutionary distance suggested a certain
appropriateness to the display and, consequently, absolved viewers from
any indictment of their social conscience for participating. Such historicist
views allowed for a relative application of morality and concepts of social
justice, thus making the exhibit an appreciable cultural display. This interpretation was quickly disseminated throughout the broader nation as the
New York Times reprinted the article one day after it appeared in the *St.
Louis Post-Dispatch*.[62]

While Moro slavery offered a kind of nostalgia for taboo historical institutions, nothing titillated American imaginations more than the
seeming eroticism of Moro polygamy. Recent scholarship has produced
a large corpus of work exploring the linkages between gender, sexuality,
and empire, with sexuality providing a central "mediating term" in the
production of imperial discourse.[63] The Moro experience at the St. Louis
World's Fair is certainly no exception to this body of work. As in the
case of Moro slavery, there was an initial outpouring of indignation over
the acquisition and treatment of plural wives. Early reports to the Philippine Commission described the cruel practices of child trafficking and
wife buying for purposes of polygamy.[64] The 1903 census was equally
offended: "Polygamy is universal among them. The Koran permits four
legal wives, but frequently all except one are slaves. . . . Wives are practically bought, the suitor paying an amount agreed upon to the family of
the bride."[65]

Even up until 1904, colonial officials continued a vehement assault
on polygamy in Moro Province, long after they had softened their stance
on slavery. "The Moros [are] proud, suspicious, and fanatical," stated one
report of the Philippines Commission. "From time immemorial they
had practiced polygamy; they had been accustomed to make raids upon

other non-Christian tribes for the purpose of replenishing their stock of slaves."[66] Even courtship among them was a form of simulated or actual slave raiding, accompanied by a ceremonial "carrying off of the bride" to the husband's village.[67] Such misogynistic circumstances allegedly bore a terrible toll on Moro women. "Children wear little or no clothing in their homes," reported the 1903 census; though it was "not unusual to see the Moro women ornamented with rings and bracelets, the work of the native smiths who are skillful in molding brass and precious metals." Despite these ornamental trappings, "they cannot be said to be cleanly. Their houses and surroundings are often in a filthy condition. The people fall far short of the standard of Mohammed, with whom cleanliness was said to be the foundation of religion. . . . The food is prepared by the women in an exceedingly simple kitchen, which consists of little more than a diminutive fire over which one or two pots are placed. Cooking is frequently done beneath the house, or upon a small mound of earth on the floor of the living room."[68] The degradation of their domestic spaces infiltrated more than their surroundings, however, and also appeared to take a terrible toll on their physical bodies. "Moro women spend much of their time indoors," continued the census, "and are consequently more or less anemic, their lives averaging less than those of the men. They marry young, give birth to large families, and age rapidly."[69] Such observations are consistent with American Orientalist tendencies to probe and exhibit the domestic and interior spaces of the colonized. Inadequate sanitation, insufficient nutrition, poorly constructed housing and possessions, and other forms of nonmodern living contained both the rationales supporting paternalist colonialism and the inherent terrors of biological and racial pathogens that threatened the white masculinity underpinning such paternalism.[70]

As in the case of Moro slavery, however, the World's Fair demonstrated a remarkable ability to sanitize taboo sexual behaviors for mass consumption. As Barbara Kirshenblatt-Gimblett observed, museums and exhibits "served as surrogate theaters during periods when [regular] theaters came under attack for religious reasons."[71] One might also add social conscience and political expediency to these reasons for repressing sexually suggestive material in public. Nevertheless, when this material was presented within an educational or scientific context, audiences could indulge in proscribed behaviors with little guilt or social stigma. This exceptional latitude created an explosion of sexually charged activities and images at the fair. While passing through the midway, patrons could purchase aluminum cards, small booklets, or glossy photographs of bare-breasted women, up-skirt peeking, a boy urinating from a dock, and other scandalous images.[72] Thousands flocked to "Mysterious Asia," where, for the price of admission, one could witness belly dancers, erotic art, and exotically clad women.[73] The presence of erotic images was so ubiquitous that the Asiatic Theater was bound under terms of its concession not to allow explicitly "naughty" dances.[74] Islam was particularly provocative in this regard, as "many varied interpretations of Islam emerged from the exhibitions." Like the garishly decorated booths and storefronts, Islamic exhibits displayed ornate architecture, beautiful paintings, and artistic calligraphy as a testament to "a distant historical past [and] a golden age of cultural development." Yet, "within [those] walls [also] lurked the decadence of harems and slavery," forbidden worlds of royalty and pleasure.[75]

Within this swirling atmosphere of suggestive and explicit sexuality, Moro polygamy commanded a remarkably high level of curiosity and even admiration among fairgoers. This favorable interpretation of Moro sexual practice marked a sharp and abrupt departure from established colonial tropes on the subject, not only concerning its perceived immorality but also in terms of Moro masculinity. The Americans' colonial narrative of gender oppression in Moro Province was marked by a conspicuous nonrecognition of potent sexuality among Moro men. While Moro women were certainly cast as victims of institutionalized polygamy and economic commodification, very rarely was this associated explicitly with vigorous or systematic sexual impositions on the part of Moro men. In fact, throughout the records Moro men appear rather asexual in terms of explicitly rapacious or virulent sexuality. Their particular forms of masculinity were rather expressed (and indeed celebrated) in the records in a variety of outwardly asexual contexts—militant acts of war, conquest of local environments, physical forms, entrepreneurial instincts, and so on.[76] This downplay of overt indigenous sexuality contrasted sharply with the Americans' bold pronouncements of their own boundless virility in the colony. This juxtaposition seems to confirm Gail Bederman's conclusions regarding the displacement of "manliness" (character, discipline, sexual forbearance) with "masculinity" (competitive, aggressive, sexual) during the Progressive Era.[77]

This notion of the asexual Moro subject was utterly discarded, however, at the St. Louis World's Fair. American patrons and the local press became deeply enamored with highly erotic impressions of potently masculine Moro sexuality, which sometimes even served as a subtle critique for the overcivilization and feminization of modern American men.[78] In May 1904, for example, the *St. Louis Republic* ran a surprisingly quixotic profile of Datu Facundo's romantic adventures in Moro Province. The article began with a stunningly provocative comparison of Moro and American romantic masculinity: "The strenuous life of a Moro lover would be too much for even the most enthusiastic American, for the Moro, instead of killing himself, kills his rivals when crossed in love." The piece then went on to tell the story of Facundo's undying love for a young Moro maiden, a love that was vehemently opposed by the girl's family and many suitors. Nevertheless, the proud Datu "would not be disappointed or awed by combined opposition." The maiden's brother first attempted to assassinate Facundo, but the determined lover fought off his attacker, killing him in the process. Facundo then unleashed a nearly two-year-long "bloody raid of the girl's relations and suitors, ending only when all had been killed." In the wake of fourteen slain objectors, the maiden was "spirited away by her family . . . through the wildest mountain tribes," but Facundo proved similarly undeterred by the rugged wilderness. At long last he tracked them down and married his love, who subsequently accompanied him to the St. Louis World's Fair.[79]

Far from the asexual, nonpotent subject of colonial reports, Datu Facundo stood as the embodiment of American masculine aspirations at the St. Louis World's Fair. His remarkable capacity for romance, sexuality, and violence fulfilled Americans' nostalgic fantasies of a time before the civilized anemia of industrial modernity.[80] By the end of the fair many Americans and the St. Louis press were actively supporting Moro polygamy. On September 6, 1904, the *St. Louis Post-Dispatch* covered a ceremonial restoration of rank and title to a Moro named Demasanky, who "received a nipa house all his own and a big sign . . . announcing him the ruler of 13,000 people." Despite the pageantry and celebration of Demasanky's restoration, however, he was not yet a bone fide sultan. For, observed a reporter, "according to all the laws of the Moros a sultan is not a sultan unless he has a harem." Consequently, the paper blared the following advertisement: "WANTED—Six beautiful Moro women who are willing to join the harem of a sultan."[81] While it is unclear if any women actually inquired after the advertisement, the paper's purpose was undoubtedly larger than the simple acquisition of plural wives for Demasanky. The article with its salacious headline was designed as a provocation for vicarious sexual fantasy. The highly Orientalist notions of rank, royalty, and sexual privilege fueled American expectations of the exotic East. Moro polygamy also allowed for a new appreciation of the once widely condemned practice of plural marriage among American religious sects.[82] When properly exhibited within a "valid scientific context," such practices became morally relative and a matter of education, cultural exchange, and cosmopolitan understanding.

Very quickly Americans started to bridge the cultural distance between colonizer and colonized and began to imagine the real possibility of becoming slave masters and polygamists themselves. In June 1904 the *St. Louis Post-Dispatch* reported on the remarkable experiences of Arthur E. Anderson, who began his career in Boston's city architect's office. After passing the civil service examination he transferred to Manila where he served in the Bureau of Architecture under the direction of the Philippine Commission. When the Philippine Exhibit Commission initiated a contest for designs for the Philippine Village at the St. Louis World's Fair, Anderson collaborated with a colleague named Guy Mahurin to create a winning plan. By October 1903 Anderson had already shipped in over forty-five hundred tons of materials for his masterpiece, which ultimately earned him a "Medal of Honor with Diploma of Gold Medal."[83] Although Anderson had never been to Mindanao nor met any Moros during his time in the islands, his Philippine Village design placed him in accommodations adjoining the Moro Village. The Moros and Anderson took an immediate and profound liking to one another. Anderson became deeply interested in the Lanao Moros' culture and frequently invited them into his home, allowing them to explore his possessions and experience a bit of American culture. The mutual respect and affection grew so deep that the Lanao Moros proclaimed Anderson a sultan and offered him the royal name of Abugaton, in honor of a revered warrior and teacher.

The *St. Louis Post-Dispatch* hastily exploded with lurid speculations on Anderson's impending life of luxury and sexual privilege in Moro Province as a Moro sultan. "They offer him slaves and numerous wives and assurances of the devotion of his subjects," reported the paper, adding that Anderson "is considering the proposition with the utmost seriousness." Far from the stated democratic aims of American tutelary colonialism in the Philippines, the article suggested that Anderson could rule his subjects as a kind of benevolent monarch. "So completely has Mr. Anderson won the affections of the Moros that it is not probable that he would have any difficulty in ruling them humanely. Their simple trust in him and love for him is touching. They follow him about as docile pets follow a kind master. They are never so happy as when with him. Anything he suggests is law to them." Although the paper proposed that Anderson could serve as an enlightened despot, the conventions of his position necessarily required that his subjects be considered slaves. Yet, the article was quick to place this fact in its proper perspective as well:

> The subjects acquired in these ways would be slaves, just as the subjects of the native sultans are slaves, but their slavery is unlike that which once prevailed in this country. While the white sultan would have power of life and death over them and could keep them or dispose of them to another sultan and would be supreme over them in every particular, most of them would live in their own houses and follow their own inclinations as to how much or how little work they would do, only paying tribute to the sultan.[84]

Even when potentially practiced by an American, the nature of the exhibit had a remarkable ability to sanitize and rehabilitate slavery as an institution. What began the fair as a primitive, but curious, practice of savage colonial "others," now, in the case of Anderson, became a potentially acceptable practice for an indigenized American. This marked a sharp departure not only from Americans' socially conscious disdain for slavery but from pervasive colonial fears of cultural degeneracy and the specter of "going native."[85]

Yet, the manufactured fantasy of the exposition allowed for a kind of cultural and moral relativism among the intensely diverse cultural manifestations of human existence, sanitizing taboo practices for mass consumption. While the notion of an enlightened colonial slavery piqued the public interest, the prospect of Anderson's plural wives set the public imagination positively ablaze. As a consequence of his new appellation, Anderson was entitled to "a harem full of wives" selected "from the most beautiful girls on the island." The immediate questions were how many wives he would acquire and how such a domestic arrangement might be managed. The *St. Louis Post-Dispatch* noted that the Koran officially recognized four wives but explained that this was only for women of a certain status. There was no such prohibition for "wives of a lesser standing," which could be "an unlimited number." "He could have as many wives as he cared for," explained the paper, "just as his subjects could have as many as they were able to support. But unlike them, he would not have to ask the consent of anybody when he took a notion to take unto himself a new wife or two." In fact, "Mr. Anderson . . . will own all the female slaves in the barrio, or native town, over which he rules." Lest readers think that such domestic circumstances may lead to chaos and familial strive, the article highlighted Mr. Anderson's prerogative to exercise patriarchal discipline at his discretion. "[He] will have the right to whip his wives whenever the spirit moves him. He can also divorce them at will. All that is necessary for divorce is for him to confront one of his wives and say: 'I divorce you!' three times. With that the woman ceases to be his wife." While such patriarchal fantasies would certainly be impossible in bourgeois American society, many observers were acutely aware that there was once a place in the United States where unconventional lives thrived, where adventurers could escape the suffocating gaze of industrial modernity and its attendant social expectations. The old frontier was the last bastion of unbridled individual expression. The article fittingly ended with a profound reminder that America had again acquired such a place. "Slavery and polygamy are of course illegal," the paper ceded, "but the greater part of Mindanao is not only ruled by native custom but unexplored today."[86]

While the Moros' official designation as "semi-civilized" allowed fair officials and promoters a great deal of latitude to portray their live exhibits in a variety of different and often contradictory ways supporting US empire, it also provided a liminal space for independent American observers to paint the Moros with their own fantasies of exotic, taboo, and nostalgic practices. In this way the Moro Village provided the quintessence of a malleable and infinitely interpretable imperial discourse at the Louisiana Purchase Exposition; a "visual scape" that "created a space for a dialogue about empire that words alone could not nurture."[87] Official and counterdiscourses of savagery and civilization meandered back and forth, intertwined, separated, disappeared, and reemerged as something distinctly hybrid, collaborative, and organic. The highly contingent dialogue characterizing "semi-civilized" colonial subjects cut a wide berth for interpretation that served sharply divergent American desires. The display's free market context further punctuated and solidified these insurgent interpretations as fairgoers democratically dispersed their funds to those exhibits that specifically catered to popular yearnings for nostalgia, exoticism, freedom, escape, and indulgence. The entire exhibit was thus an exercise in negotiated power among government and civic officials, colonial subjects, the American public, and the local and national press. However, not every aspect of the Moro display was so subjective. There was also a great effort to demonstrate firm empirical evidence of the asymmetries in culture and race that ultimately justified US empire in the Philippines. Fair organizers believed that this empirical data was most clearly inscribed on Moro bodies.

3

Measuring Moros

While the fair's exhibits overwhelmingly centered on the "demotic" intellectual and cultural evolution of the world's inhabitants, "biotic" development also played a significant role in crafting master narratives of imperial necessity and dominance. Recent scholarship has convincingly illustrated the ways in which modern human bodies have become objects of knowledge and are constructed, defined, and controlled through institutional observation and scientific quantification.[1] The growing nineteenth- and twentieth-century corpus of scientific knowledge presented human bodies as a reducible set of unassailable scientific facts, which could be used to objectively taxonomize human populations and create an assumed "natural" social or political order based on biology.

In his extensive study on the construction of race during the early years of American empire in the Philippines, Paul Kramer demonstrates the critical function of imperial discourse as a catalyst for scientific race making, both at Bilibid Prison and later at the St. Louis World's Fair. Kramer also points out that despite its scientific underpinnings, however, race remained "a dynamic, contextual, contested, and contingent field of power."[2] Elizabeth Collingham similarly illustrates the volatile and discursive formation of imperial bodies within a shifting colonial landscape.[3] Despite its supposed empirical validity, the resulting discourses of scientific race inevitably problematized and unsettled the very object they sought to establish. Race making is a matter of drawing definitive lines predicated upon phenotypic credentials that can be consistently recognized, measured, and catalogued as markers of similarity or difference. However, as the modern world increasingly presented a seemingly infinite spectral manifestation of human forms, these lines of similarity and difference had to be erased and redrawn with astounding rapidity.[4] Each time this occurred, the scientific motivations, methods, conclusions, and exhibition of acquired knowledge were deeply influenced by shifting concerns over access to political and economic power, atavistic fears, colonial desires, exotic fantasies, technological innovation, and anxieties of overcivilization, among many other concerns. In this way the St. Louis World's Fair presented an unprecedented opportunity to conduct intensive qualitative studies on the diverse mass of humanity in attendance. Exposition authorities believed that comparatively quantifying various human forms at a single central location could potentially accomplish more work in a matter of months than an army of anthropologists could over years of fieldwork. American scholars could not let the opportunity pass.

Vast experiments were conducted at the Louisiana Purchase Exposition's Department of Anthropology, headed by William J. McGee. Aside from limited attendance in a one-room schoolhouse in eastern Iowa, McGee had virtually no formal education, nevertheless his intellectual curiosity and ambition were boundless. In 1881 he began work as a geologist for the US Geological Survey. As a result of his travels he was appointed lead ethnologist at the Bureau of American Ethnology in 1893. For the next decade McGee explored and documented the disappearing culture of American Indians. In 1902 he became the founding president of the American Anthropological Association (AAA). As a leader in this burgeoning field he was a passionate advocate of "amateur" scholarship. As president of the AAA, McGee publicly broke from established ethnologists such as Franz Boas, who were attempting to professionalize the field through academic credentialing. McGee established an open organization and encouraged interested parties from all backgrounds to engage in ethnological studies. McGee and Boas also differed sharply on theory. Boas frequently criticized McGee's "dogmatic cultural evolutionism," as embodied in McGee's 1899 article, "The Trend of Human Progress."[5] These differences ultimately led to McGee's ouster as president of the AAA in 1902. However, he very quickly received an appointment as director of anthropology for the Louisiana Purchase Exposition in 1903. Thus, the World's Fair presented McGee with a critical opportunity for both validation and vindication of his anthropological theories and his preferences for an inclusive approach to the discipline.

The key to McGee's vast collection of experiments was his unfettered access to a host of colonized bodies. As Gonzalez observes, anthropological knowledge fundamentally "rests on the assumed availability and accessibility of the native body. . . . [T]he native body functions as a shorthand for entire cultures and life worlds, signaling authenticity through its exhibition of pastness, difference and indigeneity. This metonymnic reduction—collapsing complex cultural histories and social landscapes into a knowable, transparent visual body—is the pedagogy of imperial anthropology."[6] However, while anthropologists at the World's Fair were certainly interested in collapsing cultural complexity into knowable visual images, they were not interested in reproducing overly simple binaries between civilization and savagery. Rather, these scholars were intent on demonstrating a nuanced and highly specific spectrum of human forms, illustrating a detailed, inclusive, and ongoing process of human evolution.

In this regard the Philippine exhibit was essential. Fair publications, private memoirs, and government reports all touted the invaluable collection of "physical types" contained in the Philippine Village's eleven hundred live exhibits. Francis hailed the Philippine exhibit as "the most impressive illustration of alien life and customs ever assembled."[7] Colonial officials in the Philippines similarly advertised the academic value of the islands' diverse inhabitants. "The study of the races of man is always of great interest," read a Report of the Philippine Commission. "This is especially true in the Philippines, where live the most distinct people, representing the greater part of the races of the globe, in some instances pure, in others mixed since very remote times. Here man presents himself with the greatest variety of characteristics conceivable, as has been noted by eminent ethnologists . . . all the races are represented in these islands."[8] Fair observer J. W. Buel similarly hailed the Philippine exhibit as "a distribution of races more remarkable for manners and variableness than is to be met with in any other part of the earth."[9]

With such a variety of "types" among the Filipinos, the Moros' designation as "semi-civilized" became particularly important. It represented a critical liminal space wherein crowds of fairgoers, who were deeply curious and ambivalent about their own status in a starkly heterogeneous modern world, could make a meaningful connection with the displays. As "semi-civilized" exhibits, Moros represented both sides of an intriguing divide. And just as with their demotic allure as both savages and recognizable subjects, Moro bodies similarly fulfilled fantasies of rugged, environmentally chiseled forms as well as the potential of refined and trained modern bodies. Moros once again provided a middle ground that softened the stark binary of civilization and savagery and allowed for a space where regular Americans could explore their own modern habitations and calibrate themselves to a rapidly changing world.

Quantifiable Humanity

While McGee's anthropometric experiments relied heavily on the accessibility of colonized bodies, Caucasian American bodies were also essential. In order to establish valid empirical comparisons along the spectrum of biocultural evolution, anthropologists needed to subject middle-class white Americans to the same quantifying measurements they applied to live exhibits. Although scientific race making was often applied politically and culturally to reinforce binary separations of various peoples, predominant biological theories of race at the turn of the century did not recognize these binaries. Rather, race was seen as a vast spectral bell curve, with the vast majority of human beings falling somewhere in the middle. Humanity was composed of varying developmental manifestations of a single form. Thus, in a sense, civilized and savage bodies were intimately connected, with each revealing essential information about the other.

Early twentieth-century biologists largely accepted the false biogenetic notion that "ontogeny recapitulates phylogeny." According to this evolutionary law, all animal embryos recapitulated the evolutionary phases of their species as a whole until arriving at the latest stage of evolutionary development shortly before birth. Therefore, all human beings necessarily passed through various stages of biological primitivism before arriving at their racially determined developmental climax in utero.[10] This had two critical implications for those at the fair. First, it meant that white middle-class Americans still had vestiges of primitivism and savagery lurking within their genetic material and had in fact experienced these developmental stages, however briefly, during their gestation. Second, all live exhibits at the exposition had the potential for and a marked path toward evolutionary development and, therefore, were not definitively separated from fair patrons in their humanity. While such proximity could potentially provoke atavistic fears of the devolution of the white race or "going native," most fair participants viewed anthropometric experiments as an ideal intersection between metropolitan and colonial populations, where fairgoers could make a personal connection to both the exhibits and the scientific methodologies that ordered and validated their status in the world. As Tony Bennett observes: "For the liberal and reforming currents in [the] nineteenth-century . . . the attraction of Darwin's thought was that, in loosening up the fixity of species by allowing that one form of life might evolve into a higher one, it made the boundaries between them more permeable. . . . [T]he revised forms of ranking human life made possible by evolutionary theory gave rise to the possibility that, in principle, all populations might be inscribed within a programme of progressive self-improvement."[11]

The Department of Anthropology was located in Cupples Hall on the campus of Washington University. The main floor consisted of a vast exhibit depicting the "evolution of man," with an emphasis on technological innovations in warfare, production, and domestic use.[12] The display was conceived with the idea of demonstrating a spectrum of "all the world's races, ranging from the smallest pygmies to the most gigantic peoples, from the darkest blacks to the dominant whites, and from the lowest known culture (the dawn of the Stone Age) to its highest culmination in the Age of Metal, which . . . is now maturing in the Age of Power."[13] However, the exhibit left one enduring question unanswered: why the stark disparity in human development? Why the difference? McGee and his associates attempted to answer this question in a highly systematized set of scientific experiments conducted in the basement of Cupples Hall, which housed the Departments of Anthropometry and Psychometry.

By 1904 both anthropometry and psychometry were widely used in both academic and popular culture. These scientific successors to phrenology, which had been largely discredited by the twentieth century, were used to "identify criminals, women who would make good wives, good athletes, and potential artists or geniuses."[14] By taking a comprehensive and quantitative approach to human forms and basic cognitive abilities, scholars felt they could establish valid taxonomies of human types, racial and otherwise. McGee solicited a Harvard graduate psychologist and assistant professor at Columbia University, Robert S. Woodworth, to head the Departments of Anthropometry and Psychometry, with the assistance of his top graduate student, Frank G. Bruner. Woodworth was a longtime disciple of G. Stanley Hall's teachings on childhood development and evolutionary theory. His own work in psychology earned him enthusiastic recommendations from such luminaries as Ales Hrdlicka, curator of physical anthropology at the Smithsonian Institute, James McKeen Cattell, chair of the Psychology Department at Columbia University, and Franz Boas. McGee instructed Woodworth and Bruner to base their methodologies on William H. R. Rivers's work at Cambridge University, which consisted of a new system of sensory testing in controlled psychological laboratories at Cambridge University and London's University College. Prior to the exposition Woodworth and Bruner honed these methods by testing New York immigrants.[15]

In the months leading up to the fair McGee attempted to educate the public on both the purpose and procedures of his laboratory. In a lengthy piece in the *World's Fair Bulletin* he touted his department's "systematic studies of both the physical and the mental characteristics of mankind," which would conclusively establish "in a quantitative way the effects of civilized and enlightened life on the physical system." Participants could expect anthropometric measurements including "stature, arm-spread, girth, weight, head form, facial angle, attitude of eyes, chest expansion, girth of body and limbs, relative lengths of limbs and body, rates of pulsation and respiration, with determinations of digital and joint movements, [and] form and expression of features." Photography and plaster casting would also be available for instructional and comparative purposes. Psychic measurements included "sensitiveness to temperature, delicacy of touch

and taste, acuteness of vision and hearing, and other sense reactions . . .
[the] power of co-ordination as expressed in rapidity and accuracy of
forming judgment. . . . color-blindness, [and] imperfect hearing," all to
scientifically ascertain "the relative prevalence of sense defects in the different races and culture stages."[16]

In addition to formal testing McGee allowed a number of side experiments, including a study of bare feet versus shod feet that was conducted
by a local St. Louis podiatrist named Hoffman.[17] On May 16, 1904, the
Department of Anthropometry and Psychometry formally opened to
the public. Visitors flocked in by the tens of thousands. Officials tallied
as many as three thousand patrons per day with more than twenty-five
thousand cycling through per week during the month of June. McGee
later estimated total attendance at one and a half million during the entire
fair.[18] Woodworth and Bruner were able to quickly compile measurements
on more than two hundred white, middle-class adults, which served as
a benchmark standard for subsequent comparative analyses with other
groups. Despite its scientific underpinnings, Woodworth's laboratory
exuded a carnival-like atmosphere. As one participant observed, "Woodworth's exhibit room for noting the physical characteristics of his World's
Fair visitors reminds one of the penny-in-the-slot parlor, where we may
test our punching ability, our lung power, weigh ourselves, etc. Here, you
blow; here, you are weighed. Here, your reach is measured; there, your
strength of grip is determined."[19] Psychometric experiments proved particularly popular. Woodworth had developed a kind of puzzle box that
measured progressive problem-solving abilities relative to various animals
and, later, various ethnic groups. Tourists could measure their completion
times, gauge their relative intelligence, and leave the exhibit with a scientifically validated souvenir affirming their evolutionary status. One jour-
nalist for the *Cosmopolitan* took special delight in the psychometric tests:

In the department of Psychometry tests will be made of the quickness of
mind of these various races. [An] ingenious apparatus has been invented to
show their intelligence, and these tests are begun with the monkey and go on
up to the highest development of man. One of these, which the writer had
the opportunity to try, requires one hundred efforts before the average monkey becomes proficient. It was with a feeling of pride that the writer operated the apparatus successfully the first time, showing, according to Doctor
McGee one hundred per cent greater efficiency than the ordinary monkey.[20]

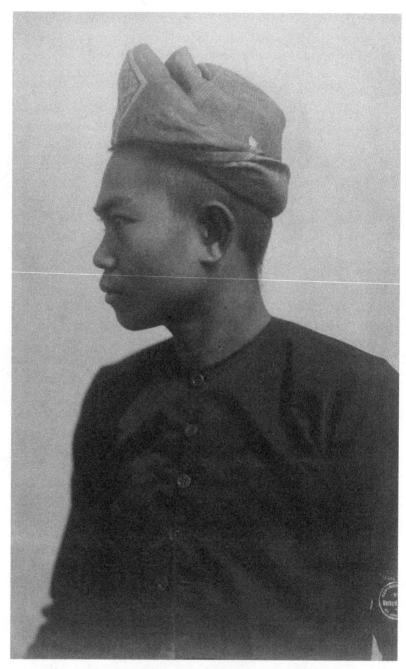

Fig. 3.1. Profile photo of a Moro man

Fig. 3.2. Profile photo of a Moro woman

While such examinations could be entertaining, they also inevitably produced anxiety. However, there are virtually no accounts of failure to be found in any official or unofficial records, suggesting perhaps that, despite its apparent scientific objectivity, Woodworth's department was most likely a set of carefully constructed, scientifically couched affirmations designed to attract patrons and give them a positive experience.

Within a few days Woodworth and Bruner began testing various live exhibits and nonwhite subjects to create a tangible racial "hierarchy of strength, intelligence, [and] dexterity" wherein observers could locate themselves in the vast panorama of human evolutionary development.[21] Woodworth focused much of his time on Filipinos, who represented a large majority of native subjects tested in the Department of Anthropometry and Psychometry.[22] His experiments were designed ostensibly to circumvent and negate cultural differences, thus preserving the methods' scientific objectivity. As one reporter observed: "Doctor Woodworth has designed a piece of apparatus by which the keenness of sight of the savage races will be tested without bringing in the element of language." Thus, it was assumed that native subjects could not compromise the scientific process through mistranslation. Yet, perhaps ironically, the entire premise of Woodworth's experiments on vision was predicated on a false understanding of native language. An article in the *St. Louis Republic* explained: "It is a known fact that in the vocabulary of savage tribes there is no word for the color blue; this has led to the belief that savages do not see the color blue, and the supposition has been strengthened by many experiments."[23] This was certainly not the case for Filipino dialects spoken at the fair, which commonly used both indigenous and Spanish terms for the color blue.[24] Yet, despite these and other misperceptions, Woodworth persisted in the examinations.

In the end the Department of Anthropometry and Psychometry arrived at somewhat unexpected conclusions. Rather than establishing a definitive hierarchy of physically based developmental differences among the races, both Woodworth and McGee ultimately found no discernible difference on a mass scale, particularly concerning color vision and manual dexterity, the two primary topics of experimentation.[25] Woodworth's assumptions and measurements of color blindness ultimately revealed that "color sense is probably very much the same all over the world."[26] He also found the same to be true for "cheirization," a belief that higher evolution could be determined by the development of a subject's forearms and coordinated dexterity.[27] After thoroughly testing groups of Filipino, Native American, and Caucasian subjects, Woodworth confirmed that his experiments did not reveal any particular connection between whiteness, right-handed dexterity, and advanced civilization. "The degree of right-handedness has been asserted to vary in different races," he explained, "and the favoring of one has been interpreted as conducive to specialization and so to civilization. We were, however, unable to detect any marked difference in the degree of righthandedness in different races."[28]

While these findings might appear to undermine the structure and purpose of the exposition at large, the lack of documented biotic difference among test subjects was actually a welcomed affirmation of McGee's theories concerning the primacy of culture and technology in determining evolutionary status over gross biology. As McGee wrote in his 1905 report on the exhibit to *Science*:

> When the world's peoples are classified by culture-grade, or in terms of progress from the lowest to the highest stages, it at once becomes manifest that they are arranged in accordance with mentality, knowledge and cerebral capacity, and measurably (with a few apparent exceptions) in accordance with general physical development, including strength endurance and viability. . . . [A]ll mankind are closely bound in a potential if not actual community of thought, sentiment, aspiration and interest. . . . [T]he world's peoples are united in solidarity of growing independence in which the less advanced may profit by association with the more advanced, and all may indeed, must progress toward higher and higher intellectual advance and toward more and more complete conquest over lower nature.[29]

Hence, although McGee believed anthropometric and psychometric measurements could determine "human types" through quantifying phenotypic and cognitive differences, those measurements and differences were ultimately and merely a consequence of exposure to primitive or advanced culture. The relative proximity or familiarity of the live exhibits to white middle class Americans was not as rare or disruptive as one might think. Although fair patrons eagerly sought out exotic, sexualized, or violent tropes among the live exhibits, there also seemed to be a certain recognition that much of what they saw was staged and that the performers led basic human lives outside of the performance. This familiarity was a part of virtually all formal exhibitions of colonized Filipinos going back to the first display of colonized subjects at the 1899 Greater American Exposition in Omaha, Nebraska, where visitors failed to see anything remarkable or exotic about the Filipinos on display.[30]

The same reaction was prevalent at the Louisiana Purchase Exposition. The St. Louis press overwhelmingly advocated for fidelity and support in Caucasian/Filipino interracial marriages, for example.[31] And though there was a violent controversy concerning the fraternization of Filipino Scouts with white women, both the *St. Louis Post-Dispatch* and the *St. Louis Republic* ran articles defending the Filipino soldiers.[32] The St. Louis press also eagerly advertised for interracial adoption.[33]

This tendency to see a common humanity between observer and observed certainly extended to the Moro exhibit. Despite numerous articles highlighting savagery and violence, fair publications and news reports were also quick to comment positively on the Moros' bodies and minds. In the early months of the fair, the *St. Louis Post-Dispatch* published a lengthy piece describing the Moros' "copper-brown" skin and average height, concluding that "Moro children are a sturdy lot" and that "Moro girls are oftentimes very pretty."[34] *The Official Handbook of the Philippines* described Moro bodies as "well developed physically," with a dark complexion, "abundant straight black hair," and "small, black, animated eyes."[35] Both official and unofficial accounts of the Philippine exhibit similarly regarded the Moros as demonstrably "the most intelligent of all the tribes inhabiting the Island."[36] Such quantitative physical and mental assessments were not unique to the fair. American military officials and ethnographers had taken great care to document the Moros' bodies during the early years of colonization. The 1903 colonial census, for example, recorded detailed observations of the Moros' "physical characteristics" including "complexion," "hair," and physical build. "They are somewhat taller than the average Filipino," recorded the census, "straight and well formed, and often strong and stockily built, with well-developed calves."[37]

Although Moro bodies were routinely quantified in a variety of contexts, the real measure of the Moros' physical prowess was to be established in a grand athletic spectacle known as "Anthropology Days." McGee felt that, by testing native bodies in motion, his anthropological theories of human development could at last find definitive validation in an impressive fashion. With the 1904 Olympics as a backdrop, McGee hoped the Anthropology Days would provide an undeniable comparison between "savage" and "civilized" athletes, thus diminishing emphasis on biological development and endorsing culture and technology as the primary measure of human difference.

Anthropology Days

The 1904 Olympic Games marked a key feature of the fair's grand display of human evolutionary progress. The Games of the III Olympiad were the first to be held in the United States. Because of the disruption of the Russo-Japanese War, 526 of the 650 participating athletes were American citizens. Thus, the games were almost exclusively an American showcase for athletic prowess. The United States took home 239 of the 280 medals awarded. The next closest nation was Germany with 13 medals. The 1904 Olympics, however, were much more than a mere symbol of national pride. The Olympic Games were meant to demonstrate the apex of modern man's physical development. Millions of years of evolution could now be accurately measured and exhibited in terms of strength, speed, endurance, and dexterity. In addition to the Games' celebration of achievement, the 1904 Olympics also signified an emerging lifestyle of physical fitness designed to stave off degeneracy and maintain physical "superiority." As Mark Dyreson notes, "The [1904] Olympic games became an American exhibition of the gospel of the strenuous life."[38]

In an effort to institutionalize this ethos of physical fitness at the Louisiana Purchase Exposition, a great deal of investment and emphasis was given to the Department of Physical Culture. During the fair's early planning phases the exposition board of directors specifically called for a display of "man in his hours of recreation, his exercise, his games and his sports." The Department of Physical Culture would provide a context "in which man, his intelligence having reached its supreme point, is able to treat himself as an animal, realizing that his intellectual and moral constitution require a sound physical body to prompt them to the proper performance of their functions."[39]

James Edward Sullivan served as both the primary organizer of the 1904 Olympic Games and chief of the Department of Physical Culture.

Sullivan was an obvious choice. As a former athlete, referee, and sports-writer, Sullivan became an advocate for reviving the Olympics, and worked with Pierre de Coubertin to create the first modern Olympics in Athens in 1896. He later became director for the US Department of Physical Culture at the Paris Exposition of 1900 and director of athletics at the Pan-American Exposition in 1901. Despite his deep investment in the international games, Sullivan was profoundly passionate about local amateur athletics as well. In 1886 he was elected president of the Pas-time Athletic Club of New York and later became a primary founder and president of both the Amateur Athletic Union and the Outdoor Recre-ation League.[40] In addition to state-of-the-art athletic facilities at the St. Louis World's Fair including a 17,000-square-foot gymnasium valued at $150,000, a 760-foot athletic field with track, and stadium seating for 25,000, Sullivan also endorsed and organized athletic events at all levels of St. Louis society.[41] Schoolchildren and local residents were encouraged to participate in athletic days, YMCA basketball tournaments, football games, as well as archery and golf contests.[42]

Like Theodore Roosevelt, G. Stanley Hall, and other thinkers at the time, Sullivan was deeply concerned with the potential deleterious con-sequences of technology, mechanization, and overcivilization on the sup-posed physical supremacy of Americans. He explained the philosophy and objectives of his exhibit:

> The trend of population is toward the cities; and in the city and everywhere else the machine is robbing man of the exercise of labor. The brain, through its infinitely numerous and varied creations of invention and device, is doing the tasks formerly left to the body and the body is warping with inaction. An adjustment is demanded. . . . The growing popularity of athletic sports which have in late years been so generally encouraged by the colleges and which are so rapidly spreading through the public schools of this country is a reflection of the increasing conviction in the minds of bodily weakened, perhaps desk bent fathers, that their offspring must be encouraged to grow up strong. . . . The presence of interest and enthusiasm in physical vigor and comeliness and athletic achievement is the mark of wholesome civiliza-tion. . . . It further means that great essential to health, morality. Physical training represents a fundamental movement of moral reform. It comforts youth and manhood with vital facts, directly illustrates cause and result,

shows the drain of vice, bad habits, neglect and irregularities upon the body. The sound body is the safest guardian of morality and of civilization—so agree teachers and philosophers as well as physicians. Physical Culture is the medium of sound organs and wholesome impulse.[43]

Sullivan believed that proper robust physical exercise could provide a kind of antidote for the social and physical costs of industrial modernity. However, unlike Roosevelt or Hall, Sullivan did not indulge in a nostalgic longing for the physically demanding circumstances of the nineteenth century. Rather, his gaze was firmly set toward the future and a celebratory embrace of scientific modernity. As the *World's Fair Bulletin* recorded: "One of the most advanced features of the Department of Physical Culture was the bringing together of unquestionably the most scientific body of physical training experts that has ever been assembled." The results were "many thousands of splendid specimens of physical manhood" unprecedented in human history.[44] For the average American, however, the professionalization of athletics signified not only the ultimate potential of bodily development but also a realm of physical training that was certainly beyond the financial or corporeal realities of most. In this way, the physical stature and development of professional athletes could seem as foreign, exotic, and distant as many of the savage displays but with the added feature of making observers feel inferior rather than superior. Thus, the exposition of "physical manhood," while forward-looking and race-affirming, failed to appeal to the demands of nostalgia and accessibility sought by many fairgoers.

Sensing this deficiency and eager to promote their own exhibits, McGee and Stephen Chapman Simms, the director of the University of Chicago's Field Museum of Anthropology, began to actively publicize the exceptional, environmentally induced natural athleticism of the savage exhibits.[45] This promotion marked a sharp departure from McGee's previous conclusions regarding civilization and physical development, nevertheless his exposure to the live exhibits had impressed upon him the raw physical potential of the "savages" due to their strenuous lives of technological deprivation.[46]

The Moros were especially important for McGee's case. Filipino Muslims enjoyed a long-standing reputation for physical prowess and

uncommon feats of strength and athleticism. As early as 1900, ethnological accounts included in Philippine Commission reports described the
Moros' superhuman physical abilities:

> Conspicuous for his sobriety, he [the Moro] nourishes himself with a hand-
> ful of rice, with the fruits which he gathers in the forests, the herbs of the
> plain, and the little fish of the streams . . . when he is afloat [he] satisfies his
> thirst with sea water. Extremely agile, he quickly ascends the mountains,
> climbs the highest trees, crosses the deepest and thickest mangrove swamps,
> fords the torrents, leaps across the small streams, and lets himself drop with
> the utmost coolness from a height of 15 or 20 feet . . . he swims like a fish,
> so that the crossing of a river, although be it wide and swift, is for him the
> most simple and natural thing in the world.[47]

News reports from Moro Province also gushed over the Moros' uncommon
"manliness."[48] Even military officials engaged in sensational accounts of
Moro athleticism and physical stamina. Colonel Owen Sweet, command-
ing officer of the Third Military District of Moro Province (1899–1901),
described the Moro as "the most perfect of aquatic beings. . . . He can no
more drown than can a fish. There is no record of a drowned Moro. He
can dive to the bottom of the sea at depths of from twenty-five to one hundred feet."[49] Major Hugh Scott, former employee for the Bureau of American Ethnology of the Smithsonian Institution and Military Governor of
the Sulu Archipelago (1903–1906) offered an even more sensational
assessment:

> The Moro appears to have a nervous system differing from that of a white
> man, for he carries lead like a grizzly bear and keeps coming on after being
> shot again and again. The only weapon that seems adequate to melt him im-
> mediately in his tracks is a pump-gun loaded with buck-shot. One Moro
> of Jolo was shot through the body by seven army revolver bullets, yet kept
> coming on with enough vitality and force to shear off the leg of an engineer
> soldier, more smoothly than it could have been taken off by a surgeon.[50]

The St. Louis press was quick to pick up on the Moros' physical and
athletic potential. "Moro children are a sturdy lot," reported an article in
the *St. Louis Post-Dispatch* in May 1904, "their grand health and strength
being due to the outdoor life they live. . . . They are expert swimmers, their

skill in the water equaling that of the famous surf swimmers of the Fiji islands."[51] By July the Moros had emerged as the premiere athletes among the live exhibits. The St. Louis press raved about the Filipino Muslims' multifaceted talents. "Both at rowing and swimming the Moros cannot be surpassed," argued one article, "the Moro crews strike the water with the paddles with as much precision and regularity as a well-trained American crew." Their athletic abilities were not limited to water sports, however. Observers found that "the Moros can easily send the [sipa] ball 50 feet in the air with a kick from the soles of the feet that shows but little effort on the part of the kicker. . . . Bulong, a thirty-year-old Moro, is the star player of that tribe in the Philippine village. He has a remarkably keen eye and approaches the ball in a swift but steady manner, seldom failing to strike the ball before it hits the ground." The Samal Moros, which were considered "the most proficient in an athletic way," were particularly impressive.[52]

The Moros' natural inclination toward sports and the ease with which they performed athletic feats would seem to confirm McGee's claims, particularly since Moro aptitude for body control, strength, and speed came without institutionalized sports programs, standardized training, or proper facilities. Nevertheless, Sullivan took umbrage at McGee's claims and proposed a series of athletic competitions to scientifically quantify "savage" athleticism. Sullivan later wrote: "[After] several conferences with Dr. WJ McGee, Chief of the Department of Anthropology, in relation to the athletic ability of the several savage tribes, and owing to the startling rumors and statements that were made in relation to the speed, stamina and strength of each and every particular tribe that was represented at St. Louis, it was decided to inaugurate a two-days athletic meet."[53] The grand experiment was afoot.

Throughout July and into August 1904 McGee, Stephen Simms of the Field Museum of Chicago, and Luther Halsey Gulick, founding superintendent of the International YMCA Training School's Department of Physical Education and future cofounder of the Camp Fire Girls, set about organizing a grand athletic meet known as "Anthropology Days" or the "Special Olympics." Their primary tasks were to recruit suitable athletes and determine appropriate events. McGee was convinced that Filipino, and particularly Moro, participation was key. He sent a pressing letter to the chair of the Philippine Exposition Board, W. P. Wilson, requesting the

Filipinos' participation. "The program cannot be made a success with-out . . . the entry of our Filipinos," he urged.[54] After a somewhat tepid response McGee wrote Wilson again a few days later, this time with more urgency. "My feeling is that if you decide to participate the feature will be a success," he pleaded, "but that if your decision is negative it would hardly be worth while for the rest of us to proceed."[55] Recruiting was particularly difficult since amateur requirements forbade offering cash sti-pends or prizes to native participants. Nevertheless, at least five Filipino "live exhibits" agreed to take part. Three of the five were Moros (Mande Cochero Somdud, a Samal Moro, and Timon Samindud and Lanale Teman Samdude, both Lanao Moros).[56]

Through careful examination Simms selected fifteen events that he believed would best demonstrate speed, strength, and agility.[57] He also selected the events based on perceived universal or natural human incli-nations and abilities, such as running, jumping, throwing, and climbing, which eliminated highly specialized events like pole vaulting and, much to the dismay of the Moros, swimming. Archery provided the one excep-tion to this rule. Simms felt that by keeping the events basic, subsequent measurements and comparisons with Caucasian athletes would retain their validity. As the Anthropology Days approached, native athletes were given no formal explanation, instruction, or coaching on the various events aside from a brief observation of the official Olympic trials. On the actual day of competition each event and its rules were explained in English and briefly demonstrated by Dr. Martin Delaney of St. Louis University. The athletes were then sent forth to compete. As could be expected, the games were a disaster. Participants did not fully understand when to commence, when to stop, how to win, or indeed, the very notion of Western competitive sports.[58] The resulting measurements were decid-edly poor. The Moros' performance was disappointing as well. Only two of the three Moros managed to place in any event. Samdude finished sec-ond in the 100-meter dash and third in the 120-yard hurdles, while Timon placed first in the 25-foot javelin throw for accuracy.[59]

Sullivan immediately unleashed a blistering and boastful response to the supposed failure of Anthropology Days in *Spalding's Official Athletic Almanac*, which he edited. "We have for years been led to believe," he admonished, "from statements made by those who should know and from newspaper articles and books, that the average savage was fleet of foot, strong of limb, accurate with the bow and arrow and expert in throwing the stone. . . . [However] the events at St. Louis disprove these tales . . . the savage is not the natural athlete we have been led to believe." Sullivan further reveled in the embarrassment of his purportedly discredited colleagues: "They certainly expected a great deal more from the savages who competed in the Anthropology Days than events proved. . . . Lecturers and authors will in the future please omit all reference to the natural athletic ability of the savage, unless they can substantiate their alleged feats."[60]

For Sullivan, the proximity of native participants in form and substance to American athletes undoubtedly fell within Homi Bhabha's theories regarding mimicry and mockery. As Nancy Parezo observes, for the live exhibits the "athletic competitions were performative events during which Native demonstrators had a good time and poked fun at the entire undertaking."[61] Native athletes often mocked demonstrations and referees, gave minimal effort, or otherwise subverted events. Susan Brownell explains further: "The seriousness of the Olympic Games, which embodied the essence of Western civilization, could not stand up to juxtaposition against the ridiculous spectacle of untrained and unmotivated Natives halfheartedly attempting to follow the rules of the sports of 'civilized' men. Anthropology Days exposed the arbitrariness of Western sports and even Western civilization as a cultural construction. It raised the question of whether the Natives could ever be like civilized men—or worse, whether they even wanted to."[62] In other words, native participants refused to care about or hold sacred that which Sullivan considered to be the supreme feature of the fair. His ire was evident in his response.

McGee and Simms were deeply disappointed. In a series of letters Simms informed McGee that the entire exercise was not only bad science but a profound misuse of the live exhibits and a discredit to anthropology.[63] McGee felt compelled to admit a limited defeat to the *Worlds' Fair Bulletin* in the wake of Anthropology Days:

I am very much pleased with the results of the meet. It demonstrates what anthropologists have long known, that the white man leads the races of the world, both physically and mentally, and in the coordination of the two which goes to make up the best specimen of manhood, they have the "spirit of the sand." Of course, primitive peoples are experts in certain directions in which their habits and environments enable them to excel, but in all-round development no primitive people can rank in the same class with the Missouri boy.[64]

Despite this concession McGee was certain that the poor performances at the Special Olympics were not representative of native abilities. He rightly argued that native participants had not received proper training or explanation, which Sullivan also acknowledged in his report:

> Dr. McGee attributes this utter lack of athletic ability on the part of the savages to the fact that they have not been shown or educated. He thinks perhaps if they could have the use of a professional trainer for a short time that they would become as proficient as many Americans. . . . It may be claimed that these particular days did not thoroughly establish the athletic ability of the savage tribes. It was a very hard meeting to handle and many of them did not perhaps know that they were expected to do their very best.

Sullivan ultimately dismissed such claims, however, arguing that "the exhibitions given on these particular days do not speak well for them. The whole meeting proves conclusively that the savage has been a very much overrated man from an athletic point of view." Sullivan alluded to the supposed universality of the selected events. "The argument may be made," he continued, "that these savages have not been taught the art of shot putting. Quite true, but one would think that the life these men have led should enable them to easily have put this shot many feet further." In other words, strong is strong, fast is fast; in any culture. And this, he concluded, "taught a great lesson."[65]

Undeterred, McGee was determined to redeem his reputation and that of the native athletes. He immediately set about planning another athletic day for the live exhibits in mid September. But Sullivan refused to participate in any way, including the allocation of funds and forbidding the use of the terms "Anthropology Days" or "Special Olympics" for marketing purposes. McGee persisted nevertheless. He raised enough money not only to fund the games but to offer financial inducements to athletes in the sum of twenty-five cents per event for participation, two dollars for first place finishes, one dollar for second place, and fifty cents for third and fourth place.[66] McGee also organized a series of preliminary training sessions to fully familiarize native athletes with the rules, expectations, and techniques of each event. The response from the Philippine exhibit, and the Moros in particular, was overwhelming. During several preliminary competitions the Moros assumed an intense spirit of competition. The *St. Louis Post-Dispatch* remarked on their efforts, observing that Bulong (a Samal Moro) and Sotonda (a Lanao Moro) "ran well" and "showed that experience would make them excellent all-around athletes," essentially confirming McGee's contention that adequate training was the key factor.[67]

On September 6, the Moros invited the Igorrotes to their village for an intertribal athletic day of "friendly competition" as a preliminary meet before the final contest. After a warm welcome from Datu Facundo and the various sultans of the Lanao region, the Moros commenced to "put it all over the Igorrotes," besting their neighbors in every single event. The St. Louis press could not help but mark the Moros' rapid progress in Western athletics. One reporter from the *St. Louis Post-Dispatch* noted how the "Moros showed that they had profited by several visits to the Stadium. They knew how to take hold of American athletics."[68] The Moros' steady improvement again exuded and affirmed their designation as "semi-civilized." Moro athletic training seemed to mediate a comfortable middle path between Sullivan's and McGee's theories of athletic accomplishment. Ethnological reports and colonial observations had established the Moros as naturally athletic, but their raw "savage" potential failed to materialize until subjected to modern scientific training, which directed the proper use and expression of their athletic abilities. This marked path of self-improvement bespoke a familiar possibility to many Americans who sought to develop their own physical bodies and, thus, merited close coverage in the popular press.

On September 16 dozens of live Philippine exhibits once again convened to compete in a tribute to the Olympic Games. Despite Sullivan's refusal to participate and the competitions' cramped quarters on the Indian School parade grounds, McGee recorded a crowd of nearly thirty thousand observers. More than three thousand paid for premium bleacher seats. Fair patrons from all over expressed a deep interest in witnessing the games. Simms once again directed careful measurements of each athletic event. Unfortunately, these records have eluded researchers.[69] However, tangential accounts suggest a staggering improvement in performance.

The Moros categorically dominated the day, winning eight out of ten events and scoring more points as a team than all other teams combined (sixty-two to twenty-six).[70] Mandae Cochero and Sumdude (both Lanao Moros) scored a total of forty-six points between them, with Cochero racking up thirty-one points all by himself. Sumdude was the highlight of the meet, however. In his final long jump attempt he once again threatened American records with a jump of nine feet, which was a full six inches shorter than a recorded jump he made earlier in the summer. The St. Louis papers were unabashedly impressed, particularly with Sumdude, who made his staggering jump "without shoes" or the "use of a toeboard." "It was a wonderful performance," exclaimed the *St. Louis Post-Dispatch*. Observers were also impressed with the overall athleticism and modern competitive spirit of the Moros collectively, who displayed a "good natured rivalry" in each event. In sum, the paper considered the "work done by the untrained Filipinos . . . to stand comparison with that of the civilized athletes."[71]

The *St. Louis Republic* also praised the Moro competitors, to whom "went the honors of the day." The paper similarly noted their intense competitive spirit and reported with delight on an incident at the end of the meet wherein Moro athletes publicly "issued a challenge to any native tribe on the Fair grounds . . . to meet them in athletic contests," except the Indians from the Carlisle School because of their extended training. The Moros' posturing was back-dropped by a "large silken American flag, which was offered to the tribe scoring the greatest number of points."[72] The victorious posing and vivid imagery could not help but convey a profound message regarding the ultimate aims of colonial tutelage and McGee's theories of native athleticism. As Francis observed, "one will readily observe that the more civilized a clan of people are the greater number of athletic sports they indulge in."[73] The Moros had once again bridged a critical gap.

Despite the massive attendance and the coverage in the press, the Moros' achievements quickly faded from official memory. No mention was made in subsequent athletic almanacs or established histories of the fair. The philosophical mandates of imperial power could not allow for such rapid and proximate achievements so early in the colonial project, particularly by those situated so close to primal savagery. Nevertheless, the Moros captivated the popular imagination, perhaps revealing the "paralyzing disjunction between the science of nature and the science of man."[74] For McGee, though he never directly credited the Moros, the September meet seemed to restore his faith in "the virile subject of human progress." In December 1905 he enthusiastically returned to his theories of demotic evolutionary development. The "course of human progress is not that of vital evolution alone," he argued in a piece in *Science*, "but one affected increasingly through the ages by activital forces arising in and with man himself." Like the Moros' assimilation to and improvement upon Western athletics, "all mankind are closely bound in a potential if not actual community of thought, sentiment, aspiration and interest."[75]

The Moros' role in the quantification of humanity at the fair served an important double function. The "semi-civilized" Moros allowed for notions of Caucasian superiority while simultaneously offering an analogy of physical and cultural improvement for all people, thus affirming the efficacy of colonial tutelage and universal human potential. In this way the Moros were embedded firmly within the central arch of human evolution rather than on its extremes. Unlike "savage" live exhibits or indeed the exceptional Olympic athletes, Moros were more akin to average American patrons. There was something comforting and familiar in this. The "semi-civilized" found a special place in the popular press and in the imaginations of fair patrons searching for analogs to their own fragile status in the vastly expanding modern world.

CONCLUSION

The Paradox of Preservation and Performative Extinction

The Louisiana Purchase Exposition formally closed on December 1, 1904. Director David Francis ended the event with a solemn proclamation, given in front of tens of thousands of spectators and punctuated with a fireworks display. Nearly twenty million visitors had come to see the fifteen-million-dollar spectacle in St. Louis. More than sixty countries and all but two states put their products and peoples on display for the scrutiny and judgment of the world. The Philippine Village was foremost among these displays. Its eleven hundred inhabitants represented half of all live exhibits at the fair.[1] It occupied 47 of the 1,272 total acres allotted to the exposition. The village cost more than one and a half million dollars, dwarfing all other American colonial displays.[2] Never had the world seen such a vested interest in the public study, description, and display of a colonized people.

Despite such an unprecedented investment in colonial exhibition and advertisement, however, many felt that the Philippine Village was "a serious political failure." In retrospect, scholars have tended to agree.

Kramer, for example, refers to the colonial exposition as the "St. Louis fiasco." He argues: "In the end, the Exposition Board was forced to surrender much of its intended narrative to inherited Fair tropes which it had scarcely anticipated." As a result, "the colonial regimes' manifold hopes for St. Louis had all crumbled."[3] Although this may have been the case for the Philippine exhibit generally, it was certainly not the case for the Moros. Rather than "surrendering" to the "inherited Fair tropes," the Moros appealed to them, inhabited them, appropriated and reappropriated them, and substantially influenced the ways in which these tropes were represented and interpreted. Similarly, Kramer claims that "the colonial government of the Philippines quickly retreated from the sponsorship of exposition displays, never again to participate as intensively or directly in such efforts."[4] This again is emphatically not the case for the Moros. Moro participation played a central role in government-sponsored and -funded expositions such as the Philippine Carnivals of 1908 and 1909 and the Manila Carnival of 1910.[5] These tremendous spectacles recapitulated the same fascinations with savagery, nostalgia for simpler times, and familiar hopes for cultural and technological modernity that had characterized the Moros' time in St. Louis. Hence, although the Philippine exhibit may have failed to meet expectations, the Moro Village largely exceeded them.

The Moro exhibit proved quite profitable financially as well. Paid admissions to the Samal and Moro Villages in September and October rose above $18,000 per month. Total gate receipts for the combined Moro exhibits during the fair totaled $67,639.04, with an additional $531.50 derived from the sale of "miscellaneous items."[6] Total costs, including construction and maintenance of the display, daily subsistence costs for the live exhibits, and salaries for both managers and Moro participants totaled $19,510.45. Thus, excluding pre-exposition expenses, the Samal and Lanao Villages realized a combined profit of nearly $50,000.[7] This, of course, excluded any personal monies the Moros acquired through tips, appearance fees, odd jobs, or charitable giving.

The Moros also achieved significant recognition in the form of formal awards and medals. The Philippine jurors of the International Jury of Awards for the Louisiana Purchase Exposition presented the Moro exhibit with eighty-four total honors. The Samal Moros were by far the most decorated, with six grand prize designations, one gold medal, two silver medals, five bronze medals, and thirty-four honorable mentions. The Lanao Moros followed with six silver medals, five bronze medals, and twenty-four honorable mentions. Datu Facundo was awarded a special gold medal "according to the part taken by [his] subjects in making the Exposition a success" and "the faithfulness of the portrayal of native huts and manner of life" in the exhibit.[8] The jurors hoped these prizes would serve as "well based encouragements" for further "special educational value" as Filipinos continued to participate in the explanation and exhibition of their culture.[9]

Considering this success, military officials in Moro Province were quick to offer official praise a few months after the fair concluded.[10] "The Moros who went to the St. Louis Exposition . . . seem to be benefited by their visit, and their influence among their friends has been good," read a Report of the Philippine Commission. "No case has been brought up to me showing an intentional wrong by any one of the Moros who visited the United States. Now, many of the influential Moros want to visit the United States, and I recommend that arrangements be made for a number of headmen and important datos to visit the States next summer. . . . A visit of this sort, I believe, would be very beneficial for this section of the Moro country."[11] Not only did colonial officials recognize the excellent conduct of the Moros, they also identified a propensity for rapid and authentic assimilation through exposure.

The idea of prolonged exposure and assimilation beyond the exposition enjoyed vigorous support among many Moros in the closing months of the fair as well. As early as October 1904 several members of the Moro exhibit expressed a desire to remain in the United States to pursue educational and financial opportunities. A. L. Lawshe, chairman of the Philippine Exposition Board, met with Taft to discuss the orderly return of the live exhibits. Lawshe noted that, although "some of the older members of the tribes are homesick and have asked to be sent home, the younger ones are anxious to remain in American, even after the close of the Exposition."[12] Six prominent Moro leaders including Datu Facundo prepared a formal petition to President Roosevelt, "praying the Chief executive of the United States and the islands in the Pacific . . . [would] graciously permit them to remain in the United States." These "six ambitious Moros . . . are anxious to stay in this country and study," reported the *St. Louis Republic*.[13] However, despite a warm meeting with the president in which Datu

Facundo presented Roosevelt with a ceremonial bolo he had used to kill three men, the Moros were unable to present their petition.[14]

By the end of November at least twelve Moros were determined to stay. They acquired a patron in Mark L. Evans, who managed the "Filipino Midgets," Juan and Martha de la Cruz. Evans assured the Philippine Exposition Board that he would act as the Moros' custodian for one year, during which time he would "pay them the same wages as they are receiving now, feed and clothe them and give them three hours schooling each day." The Moros also directly petitioned the exposition board for the same arrangement through an interpreter. Lawshe balked at the idea, however, arguing that "the natives are not familiar enough with conditions in this country to be permitted to remain." Evans challenged the government's proprietary claims by asserting that once the fair concluded the Moros were no longer under any contract and were therefore free agents. Impatient with negotiations the Moros declared through their interpreter that they were "determined to stay if they [had] to forcibly resist deportation."[15] Nine days later three young men fled the Moro Village just before departure.[16] The boys were quickly recovered, however, and all Moro live exhibits were forcibly returned to the islands via Seattle.[17]

Although the success or failure of the exhibit can be debated, the exposition of these Moros was unquestionably overshadowed by a darkly poignant supposition of inevitable demise. The very act of curating the live exhibit set in motion a process I refer to as performative extinction. On the eastern side of the Sunken Garden, in a prominent place "forming the terminus of the main traverse avenue" of the fairgrounds, sat an elaborate statue entitled "The Destiny of the Red Man." The sculpture consisted of a buffalo and five Native Americans, two men, two children, and a woman. The woman walks with great effort, bare-chested, leaning on the buffalo for support, clutching the hand of an all but naked child walking before her and pressing the wrist of her other hand to the small of her back as if in pain. To the rear of the buffalo a young Indian sits in a wolf headdress with his arm outstretched as if relating a prophesy. An older man stands in the center. He clutches a blanket around his shoulders while gazing outward with a kind of contemplative nobility. The remaining child provides perhaps the most interesting sight of all. The young girl straddles a buffalo skull. She steadies it by the horn with one hand and curiously plunges the other hand into its empty eye socket. Her expression is a mixture of interest and hope as she gropes around the animal's cranial cavity. The buffalo skull is not the only sign of morbid death, however. The entire assemblage is presided over by Death itself, perched effortlessly atop the buffalo, its hood drawn and the flaps of its robe trailing in the breeze. Behind Death a vulture waits high upon a totem pole. It sits with shoulders hunched and its head craning downward at the unknowing Indians. Adolph A. Weinmann, a German-born American sculptor, crafted the piece in 1904 specifically for display at the exposition. According to Francis, the sculpture depicted "the story of the Indians' disappearance" and testified of their "pathetic end."[18] The sculpture offered a profound symbolic lesson regarding the inevitable march of civilization and progress. It served as a sober reminder that ethnological exhibits were but fleeting shadows, preserved only by the systems and methods of modern social science. The fair was the last gasp of things that might never be seen again.

Weinmann's sculpture was a palpable focal point for extinction as a primary theme among the ethnological displays. The narrative of human evolution was cast as a progressive, accelerating process of cultural extinction culminating in ubiquitous Western technological modernity. Prior to directing the Department of Anthropology William McGee had documented and forecast the homogenizing cultural destruction of indigenous societies facilitated by modern progress. In 1899 he observed that "human culture is becoming unified, not only through diffusion but through the extinction of the lower grades as their representatives rise into higher grades."[19] McGee's designs were careful to convey this process, as the "relics of extinct peoples and civilizations were shown in amplitude to facilitate comprehensive comparisons in the process of evolution from primitive conditions."[20] However, the exposition of live exhibits differed significantly from that of inanimate artifacts. Curated objects attained an immediate sense of timeless preservation. Material items were essentially saved from extinction through careful conservation and were continually given new life through study, explanation, and of course, exposition. Live exhibits, on the other hand, were marked for extinction at the moment of their curation. The very notion that a people or culture should be curated and displayed suggested a kind of fleeting shelf life for the exhibits. As Breitbart puts it: "extinction was posed . . . in the futures of nonexistence that ethnographic displays projected for colonized peoples."[21]

This produced an odd and ironic antithesis to the act of curation itself. Rather than serving as objects of preservation, live exhibits marked a distinctive process of cultural annihilation. Human beings passed on, cultures disappeared, but with public acts of performative extinction, fading human practices could join material objects in the modern compendium of things that once were. In this way, live exhibits truly functioned as the "contemporary ancestors" of humanity writ large, which were all products of various extinctions.[22]

Fair patrons related to this destructive process in varied and unexpected ways. Modernity, although often regarded as a white, Western, primarily industrial and middle-class phenomenon, was largely indiscriminate in its purging of older things. Mechanization displaced time-honored crafts. Innovation purged entire industries. Scientific discovery demythologized traditional enchantments. And globalized perspectives replaced exceptional individualism with cold anonymity. Ethnological displays at the Louisiana Purchase Exposition not only spoke of the evolutionary journey of the live exhibits but also deeply entangled each observer in a relentless narrative of humanity as a whole, from which none could escape. As Matt Bokovoy observes: "exhibitions of indigenous peoples [served] as primitive reminders of how far white society had progressed from the past."[23] This was structurally designed to elicit celebration and a sense of racial affirmation. However, it could also provoke the opposite. Although some of white society's history was considered a "discredited" place and therefore discardable, much of it was deeply cherished.[24] The march of modernity did not accommodate such distinctions, however. The Louisiana Purchase Exposition necessarily created a kind of complicity in this destructive process, both in its creation and in its observation by all who witnessed the exposition. Its effect on fair patrons was demonstrable, and it created a profound and deeply shared "sense of urgency."[25]

Part of the allure of the fair was its "once-in-a-lifetime" quality, particularly regarding the live exhibits. As Breitbart observes: "If, as many believed at the time, the world's 'primitive peoples' would shortly die out or be assimilated into the dominant societies around them, the fair offered a final opportunity to see and record them." As a consequence, "Social Darwinists' ideas about vanishing races gave the fair's photographic enterprise a sense of urgency."[26] Both professional and lay observers at the fair felt compelled to document and preserve that which was marked for a celebratory demise in favor of higher planes of civilization. In fact the fair itself was a primary tool of this demise. It thus presents an odd sense of doubtful ambivalence among fairgoers and organizers to so desperately try to conserve what "natural law" said could not and should not be saved. To do so would necessarily confound the processes of natural progress that had produced the context for preservation in the first place. Nevertheless, the compulsion to produce visual records of things marked for extinction characterized a deep obsession with loss. As Benito Vergara argues, "the act of producing the photographs, within the American colonial narrative, is a constant reminder of death."[27]

The notion of death described here extended well beyond the physical. Modernity presented the specter of death for virtually all things that were once taken as universal and timeless. As Marshall Berman, borrowing from Karl Marx and Friedrich Engels, pointedly stated: within the milieu of industrial modernity "all that is solid melts into air."[28] The live exhibits simply provided an exotic analogy for a process that the modern world inflicted upon all of its inhabitants. As a consequence fair patrons demonstrated an intense desire to ethnographically record their own lives through acquired artifacts and visual testaments to their fleeting existence. James Gilbert has shown how fairs provided sites for "modern pilgrimages," which held "the promise of conferring authenticity upon experience" like the "older holy places" of times past. A key to this authenticity was the acquisition of material artifacts that could be curated and exhibited through various museological modalities within the home. These artifacts or "souvenirs" from the exposition "testified to the travails and pleasures of the tourist and validated the authenticity of his or her experience." Rather than mere sentimental reminders, these items provided vital evidence to "document and preserve the visitor's experiences."[29]

Photographic evidence was even more critical than material items. Artifacts required linkage and explanation to authenticate experience. Photographs, on the other hand, provided more direct evidence of presence and participation. Vergara explains: "The camera showed what was about to disappear; the very immobility of the subject in the photograph assured its state of visibility, of a certain sort of permanence, of a forestalling of disappearance (by its constant state of 'appearing'). This is why some photographs are special to us; they serve as an assurance against complete and permanent loss. Most of the time, however, they remind us that something, indeed, has been lost forever."[30] (This impulse has certainly not slackened over the past century, particularly when one considers the present deluge of selfies and inane social media posts documenting every aspect of a person's life today.) In this way the ethnographic displays were very much a shared experience. Fair patrons and organizers were rigorously curating their own lives, as they curated the lives of their exhibits, and desired to exhibit themselves as their subjects were exhibited. Although one cannot ignore or downplay the power asymmetries that structured these curations, each of them, for both colonizer and colonized, spawned from a similar urgency. It was all a desperate attempt to preserve what was about to be lost; a collective acknowledgment that all lives are ethnographic collections of artifacts and images that ultimately tell a story of loss and extinction.

In the closing months of the fair, eminent ethnologists made a series of public lectures prognosticating the probable futures of various exhibited peoples. The Moros' status as "semi-civilized" provoked varying predictions and analyses. Professor Frederick Starr of the University of Chicago, who taught courses on ethnology during the fair, characterized the Moros as "the most aggressive and civilized of any of the islanders and entirely different in every respect from any other tribe."[31] Starr predicted a future of sociocultural evolution and civilization, a triumph of colonial tutelage for a people primed for modernity. Starr later became deeply invested in the Moros' fortunes, making visits to Moros Province and sustaining a correspondence with David Barrows, chief of the Bureau of Non-Christian Tribes in the Philippines.[32]

Dr. Albert Jenks, the chief of the Ethnological Survey for the Philippines, however, calculated an opposing outcome for the Moros. In a lecture at Washington University in November 1904, Jenks told audiences that "the Moro of the present generation" had "no hope, as no policy on the part of the Government is possible except that of rigorous repression." The only possible future for the Moro people was elevation through "mixed" blood (preferably Chinese), or natural extinction through the processes of time.[33] Interestingly, despite their vastly differing interpretations, both professors predicted some form of extinction for the Moros, be it sociocultural, genetic, or natural. In any case the "Moros," so carefully curated and exhibited at the fair, were destined for annihilation.

This conclusion seems both ironic and paradoxical considering the effort and study that went into producing the exhibit. Why curate the live exhibits or their culture at all if the tide of history would soon erase that culture by natural selection? Why preserve that which had been weighed and measured as inadequate? The underlying truth of the exposition was that many, including both organizers and patrons, did not find Moro culture to be inadequate, archaic, stagnant, parochial, or savage. They, in fact, found it relevant and revelatory. The Moros reflected narratives, anxieties, fantasies, nostalgic longings, and ambitions that many Americans held dear and actively sought in their experience at the fair. The Moros were a fond reminder of what was—and a hopeful symbol of what could be.

The evident blind spot in this tale is the Moros' self-reflective view of their own culture, particularly as it was reproduced, curated, and exhibited for metropolitan populations. While direct Moro assessments are not readily available in the existing records, it is known that Moros were voluntary and active participants in virtually every aspect of the project. However, questions of cultural preservation, authenticity, and extinction may have seemed absurd to the Moros at the fair. Their efforts were likely unconscious productions and habitations of a dynamic and unquantified culture. The obsessive need to curate one's life and the lives of others is a distinctly modern phenomenon, and it comes with a consciousness that "'being in time' must be, in one sense or other, 'being in evolution.'"[34]

The acute psychological and temporal dislocations produced by industrial modernity created a melancholy sense of weightlessness and inauthenticity for many Americans. A common therapeutic response was to regard the past as "something that can be recovered in imaginative recollection, in songs, storybooks, and dreams, and in voyages to the ruins." With the advent of industrial modernity, "the past was an object both of mourning and desire, even as it remained broken and unfamiliar."[35] This increasing lack of familiarity fueled a desire to discover, define, categorize, and exhibit the world in ways that suggested recognizable and controllable subjects. As Foucault writes, "the idea of accumulating everything, of establishing a sort of general archive, the will to enclose in one place all times, all epochs, all forms, all tastes, the idea of constituting a place of all time that is itself outside of time and inaccessible to its ravages, the project of organising in this a sort of perpetual and indefinite accumulation of time in an immobile place, this whole idea belongs to our modernity."[36]

The operative phrase in Foucault's passage is "our modernity." It is a Western and modern compulsion. The notion that Moros lay somewhere outside of Western modernity was supposedly illustrated by a lack of technology, sanitation, bureaucratic government, and so on. However, commentaries on Moro primitivism were almost always essentially rooted in their alleged lack of modern consciousness rather than in a lack of material or institutional achievements. As David Barrows wrote in 1905, the Moros, and all Filipinos, existed "for thousands of years without having a life that may be called historical."[37] And for twentieth-century Americans "history [was] important as a form of consciousness in modernity."[38] However, within their "semi-civilized" evolutionary state, the Moros were free from all this. Their exhibit was touted and accepted as profoundly authentic. Their lives were rooted in tradition, belief, traceable genealogies, enduring ascetic tastes, and mastered crafts and occupations. In sum the Moros embodied all that Americans' modern melancholy and dislocation drove them to recover and enshrine. Yet the Moros' "semi-civilized" status also allowed for a surging potential for growth and triumph, the hallmarks of American exceptionalism. In this way, the "semi-civilized" Moros at the Louisiana Purchase Exposition provided the ideal subjects— unconscious practitioners of a rugged, masculine, frontier culture, brimming with potential but unburdened by the specter of melancholy, nostalgia, or irreversible loss. The "semi-civilized" enjoyed the securities and pleasures of both worlds, an increasing impossibility in modern America.

EPILOGUE

When I was a doctoral student I had the great privilege of serving as a supporting participant in a grant project known as the Philippine Youth Leadership Program (PYLP), funded by the Youth Programs Division of the Bureau of Educational and Cultural Affairs, US Department of State. Directed by Drs. Susan Russell and Lina Ong, this innovative program gathered Christian, Muslim, and Lumad youth from Mindanao and Sulu for intensive studies in interethnic and interreligious dialogue, as well as peace studies. The program took place in both the Philippines and the United States over several years. My family had the pleasure of hosting both Christian and Muslim students in our home for several weeks. I was able to accompany students on field trips, attend seminars, and participate in follow-up conferences in Mindanao. The program has enjoyed a phenomenal impact. Participants have gone on to become doctors, lawyers, politicians, teachers, community advocates, and influential policy shapers in the Philippines. I will never forget the lessons and experiences I gained through my short involvement with the program.

There is one experience in particular that came to mind throughout the composition of this book. It occurred on the eve of my dissertation defense and has rattled around inside my head in the years since. In my final year associating with the project I was able to spend a significant amount of time with a particular observer who took a keen interest in the students and the program at large. This person developed close relationships with many of the students; holding prolonged conversations about family, schooling, life goals, musical tastes, and career plans. She watched as these young Filipinos, Moros, and Lumad returned from shopping trips to Walmart or Target or Big Lots and smiled as they sported their newly acquired watches, T-shirts, and handbags. She observed their improvised karaoke sessions and watched them dance to artists such as The Black Eyed Peas, Miley Cyrus, Beyoncé, and Taylor Swift. She learned about their favorite movie idols and sports stars. She listened as they discussed the frivolous yet seemingly profound concerns shared by teenagers across the world. It was the kind of intimate immersion experience that facilitates true cross-cultural understanding, breaking down the artificial veils that complicate our fundamentally shared humanity.

In the closing days of the program, all Filipino participants came together to perform a "Philippine Culture Night." It began with a grand buffet of Filipino delicacies, after which host families, university students and faculty, and hundreds of interested patrons filed into an auditorium for the performances. In smooth succession group after group took the stage. The youths mostly performed indigenous dances to native music while dressed in colorfully patterned costumes accented with gold jewelry and the occasional feather. The audience roared approval with each act. Parents directed their children's attention with pointed fingers, while university teachers scanned their students' faces for impressions. It was multicultural learning come to life. In the midst of the festivities I sat in the back next to the observer.

I leaned over in a moment of ill-advised impulsiveness and asked out loud, "What do you think of all this?"

She received my question with furrowed brow. "What do you mean?" she asked.

I hesitated. Perhaps it would have been better to drop it. Yet I persisted. "Well," I pressed, "you've gotten to know these kids pretty well over the last couple weeks. You know they don't dress or dance like that normally. This is a cultural display. They're doing this for us. What do you think of it?"

My companion's expression turned from incredulity to irritation mingled with anger. "I can't believe you would say such a thing," she said. "This is beautiful. It is an expression of their culture and their heritage. They are kind enough to share it with us. Only a graduate student would find something wrong with that." Her last statement hung in the air. She turned her attention back to the performance. "I just can't believe you sometimes," she said again after a few seconds.

I felt the need to explain. "All I'm saying," I whispered, "is that they are doing this for our education and entertainment. I've been able to travel a few places in this world and I can honestly say I've never been asked to do anything 'American' for the education or entertainment of my hosts."

She exhaled, but that was all.

"I mean, what if you were in rural Mongolia and they asked you display your cultural heritage through a performance? What would you do?" I let the question sit while I imagined her arrayed in bonnet and petticoats two-stepping her way around the steppe or soliciting volunteers for a square dance or jete assemble.[1]

She admitted she did not know what she would do. I asked her why.

"Because," she explained, "American culture is everywhere already. Besides, we really don't even have a culture anyway. We're just a mix of everything all put together."

I smiled and apologized for bringing it up in the first place. She smiled too and the evening went back to normal.

I've thought of that conversation many times in the years since— no more so than when I was writing this book. Her final statement in particular has settled on my mind. The supposed ubiquity of American culture around the world and its equation with "global culture" necessarily implies a degree of dominance. While my companion certainly did not intend to convey any manner of Anglo-American chauvinism nor do I ascribe such motivations to her line of thinking to any degree, I could not escape the power asymmetries inherent in the notion.

If "American" culture is so ubiquitous, then Americans are in no need of discovery, definition, or exhibition, by themselves or by others. This creates an uncomfortable lack of reciprocity in which the dynamics of cultural exhibition are reduced to an asymmetrical "you dance for me, but I never dance for you; I discover, observe, define, and preserve the things of this world, but I am not subjected to those processes by others; I gaze and my gaze is not returned." I do not mean to imply that this power asymmetry is inherently sinister. Quite the opposite. As my companion noted, cultural performances are beautiful events and do serve to educate and uplift those who witness them. However, the organizers of the Louisiana Purchase Exposition were also quite explicit in this regard. Francis spoke of the "lessons beyond comparison" that were available at the fair, and he unequivocally declared their purpose to bring "together hitherto remote and unacquainted peoples," to promote "mutual respect," and to provide "an important step towards establishing that universal peace for which all right-minded people are striving."[2] Multicultural exchange and education were clearly foundational purposes underlying the fair. The same objectives underlie most, if not all, contemporary cultural presentations as well.

The notion of the United States' vague, eclectic, dilute, or nonexistent culture in my companion's response also captured my attention. A sense of weightless, inauthentic cultural identity has haunted Americans for at least a century and probably longer. In the myriad cultural performances I have attended over the past four decades I have found that the primary desire of those in attendance is to see something authentic. When I was a young man growing up in Idaho, school assemblies purported to feature "real Indians," "real Russians" from the Soviet Bloc, or "real Vietnamese" refugees. Their identities were always authenticated by material artifacts, cultural performances, or discussions of cultural difference that caused us to marvel and blush. After the assembly my classmates and I would rush the guests hoping to touch a feather, a sword, a hat, a religious object, or perhaps strike up a conversation to hear more of an exotic accent. We felt like men and women of the world. We had witnessed something "authentic" and, in turn, received an "authentic" experience. The various Philippine Culture Nights during my graduate program brought flashbacks as patrons thronged the youths hoping to feel the costumes, heft the spears, or snap digital selfies to authenticate their experiences on social media. Others bought "native" bracelets or necklaces and wore them home. Just as fair patrons more than a century ago sought to document their lives relative to something "ethnic," "traditional," or "historical," many Americans today seek out the same experiences. Material and visual evidence continues to authenticate these experiences and curate lives otherwise filled with anonymously mass-produced products and trendy but fleeting sociocultural practices and tastes.

Perhaps the most vivid and intense example of this phenomenon can be seen at Brigham Young University's Polynesian Cultural Center in Laie, Hawaii. Over the past fifty years over thirty-nine million visitors have been able to "travel through time and space as [they] experience thousands of years worth of culture from six different island nations, each with its own flavor and appeal."[3] Much like the Louisiana Purchase Exposition, patrons can meander from village to village and witness cultural dances, weddings, arts and crafts, planting and harvesting, musical performances, food production, fire making, war rituals, material culture, native architecture, and interactive linguistic tutorials. Visitors can authenticate their experiences through temporary tribal tattoos, jewelry, musical implements, souvenirs, and especially photographs. The general structure and experience are very similar to those at the Philippine Village at the St. Louis World's Fair, and patrons attend for many of the same reasons.

Of course, the glaring omission in this discussion is the motivations and participation of the indigenous subjects themselves. In their inaugural session following the 1904 World's Fair, the Philippine Legislature legally proscribed further exposition of indigenous groups. Bill no. 96 formally prohibited "under any circumstances the exhibition of the so-called infidel tribes in or out of the Philippine Islands."[4] The law was largely ignored, however, particularly during the Manila and Philippine Carnivals immediately following. By 1914 the Philippine Legislature affixed fines and penalties to those who would "exploit or exhibit tribal people."[5] Although these acts explicitly indicate a discomfort with ethnological exhibitions and imperial rule, it is worth noting that the Filipino legislators were presuming guardianship on behalf of the tribal peoples they governed and thereby claimed the rights of representation. In this way their concerns were likely akin to Vicente Nepomuceno's objections to the Philippine Village in 1904.[6]

As Kramer observes, one of the great struggles between American imperialists and Filipino nationalists was over the authority to define and represent non-Christian groups. This "imperial indigenism" morphed into a "nationalist colonialism [that] 'internalized' empire by arguing that those who were civilized among the colonized—in this case, the Hispanicized Filipino . . .—had the capacity, right, and duty to rule over those who were not civilized."[7] But what of those subjects actually exhibited, both then and now? Much like the "live exhibits" of 1904, today's ethnological displays are voluntary and frequently compensated. Participants often feel that their performances provide a rare opportunity to represent themselves and their culture directly without an intermediary to define and explain the "cultural other." As one former participant in the PYLP recently related: "We were privileged to exhibit our inherited, unique art that [Philippine Culture] night. Showcasing . . . the various wealth of our ethnic tribe to the audience from different cultures fosters acceptance, rather than division. [The] Philippines, as a multicultural country[,] has a lot to share among its people and to the rest of the world." Whatever power asymmetries may have been lurking in the structure of this particular cultural exhibit were ultimately irrelevant to this participant. She sought to tell a story about her culture—to herself, to her fellow Filipinos, and then to the rest of the world. PYLP codirector Susan Russell confirms this notion. She points out that many of these cultural performances are indeed curated in the sense that they are "frozen in time." However, the fact "that ethnic dances highlight the past rather than the present" perhaps serves to "mask the realities of those things that divide [Filipinos] ethnically and religiously . . ., and so are a safe way of celebrating differences." Recent work by anthropologist William Peterson has further shown that cultural exhibitions and performances are themselves indigenous elements that are integral to Philippine society.[8] Could the "live exhibits" of 1904 have viewed their roles in similar ways?

Hence, my earlier notion during the Philippine Culture Night that "they" perform for "us" perhaps betrayed a certain postcolonial cultural narcissism in which the legacies of empire often loom larger in the minds of former colonizing nations than they do in the minds of nations formerly colonized. It cannot be forgotten that "live exhibits" and cultural

performers are ultimately agents unto themselves, choosing and participating in representations that are independent of how observers may
attempt to objectify them. This was certainly the case for the Moros at the
Louisiana Purchase Exposition. The motivations, intentions, and methods
of that event remain more proximate than we might realize; its lessons
more relevant and its structures more enduring.

Notes

Preface

1. George E. Kessler was born in Frankenhausen, Germany, on July 16, 1862. Three years later his family emigrated to New York. He received his formal training at the University Jena in Germany. By the 1890s Kessler was designing major urban attractions in Kansas City and Memphis. Kessler later earned wide praise for his Louisiana Purchase Exposition design. See Kurt Culbertson, "George Edward Kessler Landscape Architect of the American Renaissance," in *Midwestern Landscape Architecture*, ed. W. H. Tishler (Urbana: University of Illinois, Press, 2000).

2. David R. Francis, *The Universal Exposition of 1904* (St. Louis: Louisiana Purchase Exposition Company, 1913), 50.

3. Ibid., 51.

4. Ibid., 75.

5. Ibid., 7.

6. See William McKinley, "Benevolent Assimilation Proclamation," December 21, 1898, in *Documentary Sources of Philippine History*, comp., ed., and annt. Gregorio F. Zaide (Manila: National Book Store, 1990).

7. Francis, *Universal Exposition*, 104.

8. *Report of the Philippine Exposition Board to the Louisiana Purchase Exposition* (St. Louis: Greeley Printery of St. Louis, 1904), 6.

9. Ibid., 531.

10. Francis, *Universal Exposition*, 187. See also Eric Breitbart, *The World on Display: Photographs from the St. Louis World's Fair, 1904* (Albuquerque: University of New Mexico Press, 1997), 51.

11. Michael C. Hawkins, "Undecided Empire: The Travails of Imperial Representation of Filipinos at the Greater America Exposition, 1899," *Philippine Studies: Historical and Ethnographic Viewpoints* 63, no. 3 (September 2015): 341–63.

Introduction

1. *ACT No. 514, Creating the Exposition Board. Circular Letter of Governor Taft and Information and Instructions for the Preparation for the Philippine Exhibit for the Louisiana Purchase Exposition to Be Held at St. Louis, Mo., USA, 1904* (Manila: Bureau of Public Printing, 1902), 15.

2. Ibid., 30.

3. Francis, *Universal Exposition*, 311.

4. See, for example, Vernadette Vicuna Gonzalez, "Headhunter Itineraries: The Philippines as America's Dream Jungle," *Global South* 3, no. 2 (Fall 2009): 144–72; Paul Kramer, "Making Concessions: Race and Empire Revisited at the Philippine Exposition, St. Louis, 1901–1905," *Radical History Review* 73 (1999): 74–114; Robert W. Rydell, *All the World's a Fair: Visions of Empire at American International Expositions, 1876–1916* (Chicago: University of Chicago Press, 1984); Paul A. Kramer, *The Blood of Government: Race, Empire, the United States, and the Philippines* (Chapel Hill: University of North Carolina Press, 2006).

5. See Lewis H. Morgan, *Ancient Society or Researches in the Lines of Human Progress from Savagery Through Barbarism to Civilization* (London: Macmillan, 1877).

6. W. J. McGee, "The Trend of Human Progress," *American Anthropologist*, n.s., vol. 1, no. 3 (July 1899): 407, 446–47.

7. *Report of the Philippine Commission to the President* (Washington, DC: Government Printing Office, 1901), 3:331 (hereafter cited as *RPC* with publication year).

8. See Bernard S. Cohn, *Colonialism and Its Forms of Knowledge: The British in India* (Princeton, NJ: Princeton University Press, 1996), 9.

9. Raymond Corbey, "Ethnographic Showcases, 1870–1930," *Cultural Anthropology* 8, no. 3 (August 1993): 361.

10. Tony Bennett, *The Birth of the Museum: History, Theory, Politics* (London: Routledge, 1995), 39.

11. Nicholas Thomas, *Colonialism's Culture: Anthropology, Travel, and Government* (Princeton, NJ: Princeton University Press, 1994), 111–12.

12. William J. McGee, "Anthropology," *World's Fair Bulletin* 5, no. 4 (February 1904): 4.

13. M. J. Lowenstein, comp., *Official Guide, Louisiana Purchase Exposition—Souvenir Edition* (St. Louis: The Official Guide Company, 1904), 92.

14. Francis, *Universal Exposition*, 180, 534.

15. Breitbart, *A World on Display*, 53.

16. Breitbart, *A World on Display*; Corbey, "Ethnographic Showcases"; Tony Bennett, "The Exhibitionary Complex," *New Formations* 4 (Spring, 1988): 73–102.

17. Bennett, *Birth of the Museum*, 39.

18. John E. Schrecker, *The Chinese Revolution in Historical Perspective* (Westport: Praeger, 2004), 100.

19. Rydell, *All the World's a Fair*, 2, 4.

20. Rydell, *World of Fairs*, 19; Burton Benedict, *The Anthropology of World's Fairs: San Francisco's Panama Pacific International Exposition of 1915* (London: Lowie Museum of Anthropology, 1983), 5.

21. Bennett, *Birth of the Museum*, 21.

22. Edward W. Said, *Orientalism* (New York: Vintage Books, 1979), 21.

23. Martha R. Clevenger, ed., *"Indescribably Grand": Diaries and Letters from the 1904 World's Fair* (St. Louis: Missouri Historical Society Press, 1996), 26.

24. See Ann Laura Stoler and Frederick Cooper, "Between Metropole and Colony: Rethinking a Research Agenda," in *Tensions of Empire: Colonial Cultures in a Bourgeois World*, ed. Frederick Cooper and Ann Laura Stoler (Berkeley: University of California Press, 1997); Ann Laura Stoler, "Rethinking Colonial Categories: European Communities and the Boundaries of Rule," *Comparative Studies in Society and History* 31, no. 1 (January 1989): 134–61; Stoler, *Carnal Knowledge and Imperial Power: Race and the Intimate in Colonial Rule* (Berkeley: University of California Press, 2002); as well as Frederick Cooper, *Colonialism in Question: Theory, Knowledge, History* (Berkeley: University of California Press, 2005); Thomas, *Colonialism Culture*; Craig J. Reynolds, "A New Look at Old Southeast Asia," *Journal of Asian Studies* 54, no. 2 (May 1995): 419–46; Tony Day, *Fluid Iron: State Formation in Southeast Asia* (Honolulu: University of Hawaii Press, 2002); Tony Day and Craig J. Reynolds, "Cosmologies, Truth Regimes, and the State in Southeast Asia," *Modern Asian Studies* 34, no. 1 (February 2000): 1–55; Vicente Rafael, *Contracting Colonialism: Translation and Christian Conversion in Tagalog Society under Early Spanish Rule* (Ithaca: Cornell University Press, 1988); Rafael, *Nationalism and the Technics of Translation in the Spanish Philippines* (Durham: Duke University Press, 2005); Reynaldo Clemena Ileto, *Pasyon and Revolution: Popular Movements in the Philippines, 1840–1910* (Manila: Ateneo de Manila University Press, 1979); Ileto, *Filipinos and Their Revolution: Event, Discourse, and Historiography* (Manila: Ateneo de Manila University Press, 1998); Kramer, *Blood of Government*; Patricio N. Abinales, *Making Mindanao: Cotabato and Davao in the Formation of the Philippine Nation-State* (Manila: Ateneo de Manila University Press, 2000); Abinales, *Images of State Power: Essays on Philippine Politics from the Margins* (Quezon City: University of the Philippines Press, 1998).

25. Stoler and Cooper, "Between Metropole and Colony," 4.

26. Said, *Orientalism*, 21.

27. The term "Moro" has a long and contentious history. During the Spanish colonial era it was employed as a pejorative indication of the southern Malay's socioracial difference from and inferiority to Christianized Filipinos. During this period, the epithet "Moro" embodied all the antipathies and condescension associated with the Spaniards' expulsion of Muslim "Moors" from southern Spain in the fifteenth century. During the twentieth century, however, Filipino Muslims have embraced the term "Moro" as a proud indication of their difference and unique history. They frequently refer to themselves as Moros and call their geographical sphere of influence "Bangsamoro"—the "Moro Nation." Hence, in this work I will employ the term freely, as an expression synonymous with "Filipino Muslims," "Muslim Filipinos," or "Muslim Malays" in Mindanao and Sulu, and as a collective reference to the various ethnolinguistic groups in the southern Philippines professing an adherence to Islam.

28. *Census of the Philippine Islands, 1903* (Washington, DC: US Bureau of the Census, 1905), 2.13.

29. Samuel K. Tan, *Sulu under American Military Rule, 1899–1913* (Quezon City: University of the Philippines Press, 1968), 1–3.

30. See Leonard Lewisohn, ed., *The Heritage of Sufism* (Boston: Oneworld, 1999); Hussin Mutalib, *Islam in Southeast Asia* (Singapore: Institute of Southeast Asian Studies, 2008); K. S. Nathan and Mohammad Hashim Kamali, eds., *Islam in Southeast Asia: Political Social and Strategic Challenges for the 21st Century* (Singapore: Institute of Southeast Asian Studies, 2005); Ahmad Ibrahim, Sharon Siddique, and Yasmin Hussain, eds., *Readings on Islam in Southeast Asia* (Singapore: Institute of Southeast Asian Studies, 1985).

31. Peter G. Gowing, *Mandate in Moroland: The American Government of Muslim Filipinos, 1899–1920* (Quezon City: Philippine Center for Advanced Studies, University of the Philippines, 1977), 8–9.

32. Ibid., 12.

33. See Cesar Adib Majul, *The Historical Background of the Muslims in the Philippines and the Present Mindanao Crisis* (Marawi City: Printed under the auspices of the Ansar El Islam as a background material on the occasion of its second national Islamic symposium and third foundation anniversary, 1972); Peter G. Gowing and Robert D. McAmis, eds., *The Muslim Filipinos* (Manila: Solidaridad Publishing House, 1974); Cesar Adib Majul, *Muslims in the Philippines* (Quezon City: University of the Philippines Press, 1973).

34. Daniel G. Brinton, "Professor Blumentritt's Studies of the Philippines," *American Anthropologist*, n.s., vol. 1, no. 1 (January 1899): 122.

35. *RPC* (1904), pt. 2, 571.

36. See Act No. 253 of the Philippine Commission, quoted in Michael O. Mastura, "Muslim Scholars and Social Science Research: Some Notes on Muslim Studies in the Philippines," in *Muslim Social Science in ASEAN*, ed. Omar Farouk Bajunid (Kuala Lumpur: Yayasan Penataran Ilmu, 1994), 153.

37. Ibid.

38. *RPC* (1904), pt. 2, 571.

39. Ibid., 567–68.

40. Datu Rajah Muda Mandi served as the headman of the Samal Tribal Ward at Magay, a village just outside Zamboanga. By all accounts a charismatic and "intelligent Moro of mixed Spanish and Moro descent," Mandi quickly gained the patronage of Americans eager to exercise influence in Moro Province. The rajah cooperated with American policies such as the abolition of slavery in 1900 and as a consequence enjoyed an increase in power and wealth. It is certainly likely that Rajah Mandi advised his brother to cooperate with the exhibit to further enhance his beneficial relationship with American colonialists. See *Census of the Philippine Islands* (1903), 1:554–56; *RPC* (1904), pt. 2, 586.

41. For required descriptions: "the following absolutely necessary requirements for every exhibit, namely: Name of exhibitor or establishment; locality, residence, or place of origin or production (full address); province; island; name of exhibit (common, commercial, scientific), species, variety, race, cross, sort, grade, quality; kind and class, group, department; number and quantities of exhibits; qualities, specific properties, importance attached and characteristics; full description, illustration, specifications, and photographs, etc., of exhibits; purpose, use, signification; dimensions of exhibits or necessary space required, and when ready for shipment. . . . Cost of production, or time employed; price or value (market price, export price); cost of transportation to nearest port and market." *ACT No. 514*, 32.

42. Ibid., 29–31.

43. *Report of the Philippine Exposition Board* (Washington, DC: Bureau of Insular Affairs, War Department, 1905), 27–29.

44. Ibid.

45. Gonzalez, "Headhunter Itineraries," 167.

46. Benito M. Vergara Jr., *Displaying Filipinos: Photography and Colonialism in Early 20th Century Philippines* (Quezon City: University of the Philippines Press, 1995), 119.

47. Barbara Kirshenblatt-Gimblett, "Objects of Ethnography," in Ivan Karp and Steven D. Lavine, eds., *Exhibiting Cultures: The Poetics and Politics of Museum Display* (Washington, DC: Smithsonian Institution, 1991), 415.

48. James Gilbert, "World's Fairs as Historical Events," in Rydell and Gwinn, *Fair Representations*, 77.

49. See James Clifford, "On Ethnographic Allegory," in *Writing Culture: The Poetics and Politics of Ethnography*, ed. James Clifford and George E. Marcus (Berkeley: University of California Press, 1986): 98–121; Johannes Fabian, *Time and the Other: How Anthropology Makes Its Object* (New York: Columbia University Press, 2002), 87–88. For a living "contact zone," see Mary Louise Pratt, *Imperial Eyes: Travel Writing and Transculturation*, 2nd ed. (New York: Routledge, 2007).

50. Bennett, *Birth of the Museum*, 21.

51. James C. Thomson Jr., Peter W. Stanley, and John Curtis Perry, *Sentimental Imperialists: The American Experience in East Asia* (New York: Harper and Row, 1981), 106.

52. *RPC* (1904), pt. 1, 334–35.

53. Homi Bhabha, "Of Mimicry and Man: The Ambivalence of Colonial Discourse," in *Tensions of Empire: Colonial Cultures in a Bourgeois World*, ed., Frederick Cooper and Ann Laura Stoler (Berkeley: University of California Press, 1997), 152–60.

54. Kramer's work, *Blood of Government*, provides excellent examples of the violent reactions provoked by this proximity when members of the opposite sex engage in interracial social mixing.

55. Bhabha, "Of Mimicry and Man," 154–59. See also Homi K. Bhabha, "Signs Taken for Wonders: Questions of Ambivalence and Authority under a Tree outside Delhi, May 1817," *Critical Inquiry* 12, no. 1 (Autumn 1985): 144–65.

56. See Cooper, *Colonialism in Question*.

57. Bennett, *Birth of the Museum*, 21, 26, 192.

58. McGee, "Anthropology," 4.

59. William F. Burdell, "Worth a Year at College," *World's Fair Bulletin* 5, no. 11 (September 1904): 44.

60. "Some World's Fair Lessons," *World's Fair Bulletin* 5, no. 11 (September 1904): 20.

61. Bennett, *Birth of the Museum*, 6.

62. Karp and Lavine, *Exhibiting Cultures*, 22–23.

63. Ibid., 152.

64. Spencer R. Crew and James E. Sims, "Locating Authenticity: Fragments of a Dialogue," in Karp and Lavine, *Exhibiting Cultures*, 163.

65. Breitbart, *A World on Display*, 38.

66. Ibid., 39.

67. T. J. Jackson Lears, *No Place of Grace: Antimodernism and the Transformation of American Culture, 1880–1920* (Chicago: University of Chicago Press, 1981), 5.

68. Ibid., 48. See also T. J. Jackson Lears, "From Salvation to Self-Realization: Advertising and the Therapeutic Roots of the Consumer Culture, 1880–1930," in *The Culture of Consumption: Critical Essays in American History, 1880–1980*, ed. Richard Wightman Fox and T. J. Jackson Lears (New York: Pantheon Books, 1983), 8.

69. For an engaging discussion of this particular historical development, see Benedict Anderson's brilliant chapter, "Nationalism, Identity, and the Logic of Seriality," in his volume *The Spectre of Comparisons: Nationalism, Southeast Asia and the World* (London: Verso, 1998).

70. Lears, *No Place of Grace*, 47.

71. Lears, "From Salvation to Self-Realization," 7.

72. Lears, *No Place of Grace*, 51.

73. For a detailed discussion of the various dimensions of modern insecurity, see Peter Fritzsche, *Stranded in the Present: Modern Time and the Melancholy of History* (Cambridge, MA: Harvard University Press, 2004), which provides an excellent account of a sense of temporal dislocation in modernity. See also Goran Blix, "Charting the

'Transitional Period': The Emergence of Modern Time in the Nineteenth Century," *History and Theory* 45 (February 2006): 51–71, and Richard Hofstadter, *The Paranoid Style in American Politics* (New York: Knopf, 1965), which both pursue similar lines of thought but each with particular insights. For an enlightening discussion of the shifting landscapes of gender—and masculinity in particular—in industrial modernity, see Gail Bederman, *Manliness and Civilization: A Cultural History of Gender and Race in the United States, 1880–1917* (Chicago: University of Chicago Press, 1995); Kristin L. Hoganson, *Fighting for American Manhood: How Gender Politics Provoked the Spanish-American and Philippine-American Wars* (New Haven, CT: Yale University Press, 1998); J. A. Mangan and James Walvin, eds., *Manliness and Morality: Middle-Class Masculinity in Britain and America, 1800–1940* (Manchester: Manchester University Press, 1987). For the volatile dynamics of labor and consumptions, see Zygmunt Bauman, *Modernity and Ambivalence* (Ithaca: Cornell University Press, 1991) in addition to Lears, *No Place of Grace*.

74. Jon B. Zachman, "The Legacy and Meaning of World's Fair Souvenirs," in Rydell and Gwinn, *Fair Representations*, 207.

75. Clevenger, *"Indescribably Grand,"* 28–29.

76. Chester G. Starr, "Historical and Philosophical Time," *History and Theory*, 6, Beiheft 6: History and the Concept of Time (1966): 34.

77. Quoted in Francis, *Universal Exposition*, 145–46.

78. See Nancy J. Parezo and Don D. Fowler, *Anthropology Goes to the Fair: The 1904 Louisiana Purchase Exposition* (Lincoln: University of Nebraska Press, 2007); Robert Bogdan, *Freak Show: Presenting Human Oddities for Amusement and Profit* (Chicago: University of Chicago Press, 1988); Cherubim A. Quizon and Patricia O. Afable, "Rethinking Displays of Filipinos at St. Louis: Embracing Heartbreak and Irony," *Philippine Studies* 52, no. 4 (2004): 439–44.

79. Betty Joseph, *Reading the East India Company, 1720–1840: Colonial Currencies of Gender* (Chicago: University of Chicago Press, 2004), 15.

1. Sensational Savages

1. "Some World's Fair Lessons," *World's Fair Bulletin* 5, no. 11 (September 1904): 20.

2. McGee, "Anthropology," 4.

3. Francis, *Universal Exposition*, 523, 534.

4. Kirshenblatt-Gimblett, "Objects of Ethnography," 397–98.

5. *ACT No. 514*, 29–30.

6. "Filipinos Are Preposterously Misrepresented," *St. Louis Post-Dispatch*, July 19, 1904, 1. It should be noted that, to American audiences, Filipino nationalists often claimed varying degrees of unity and separateness from the Moros, depending on circumstances. In 1900, for example, Sixto Lopez gave a rousing speech to the New England Anti-Imperialist League in which he somewhat misleadingly claimed, "even the Moros of Mindanao . . . acclaimed Aguinaldo and were prepared to recognize his government." See Sixto Lopez, *"Tribes" in the Philippines* (Boston: New England Anti-Imperialist League, 1900).

7. *Souvenir of the Philippine Exposition* (Manila Review of Trade and Price Current, 1904), 4.

8. *Report of the Philippine Exposition Board* (1905), 33.

9. Breitbart, *A World on Display*, 50, 39.

10. See, for example, "Before the Public Eye: Savagery in the Philippines," *Clinton Morning Age*, May 11, 1902; "Buried Pig with Moros; Col. Wallace, Who Devised Punishment to Prevent Religious Murders, Is in Washington," *New York Times*, December 21, 1903; "Fighting with Moros," *Omaha World Herald*, July 15, 1900; John F. Bass, "Jolo and the Moros,"

Harper's Weekly, November 18, 1899, 1158ad; "The Jolo Island," *Deseret News*, November 26, 1903; "Moro Debtors Become Slaves," *Spokane Daily Chronicle*, November 26, 1903; "Moro Rising Is Serious," *Chicago Tribune*, September 8, 1902; "Moros Swear to Die Fighting and Slay All Who Come," *Evening News* (San Jose, Cal.), May 8, 1903; "Our Mohammedan Wards," *New York Times*, March 25, 1900; "Treachery of a Moro," *New York Times*, May 27, 1902; "The Turbulent Moros," *Boston Evening Transcript*, July 13, 1903; "The Warlike Moros of Mindanao," *Argus*, May 21, 1904, 12.

11. "Fellow Tribesmen of These Moros Ambushed American Soldiers May 8," *St. Louis Post-Dispatch*, May 12, 1904: 11. See also, "The Warlike Moros of Mindanao," *Argus*, May 21, 1904, 12; "Filipinos Kill Americans," *St. Louis Post-Dispatch*, November 15, 1903, 8E; "The Bloodthirsty Moros," *National Tribune*, May 15, 1902, 7.

12. *Souvenir Visayan Village* (St. Louis: Philippine Photograph, 1904) 3.

13. J. W. Buel, ed., *Louisiana and the Fair* (St. Louis: World's Progress, 1904).

14. Vic Hurley, *Swish of the Kris: The Story of the Moros* (New York: E. P. Dutton, 1936).

15. See, for example, "Officer Boloed," *Mindanao Herald*, July 2, 1904, 2; "Juramentado in Jolo," *Mindanao Herald*, April 9, 1904, 1; *RPC* (1901), 3:373–74; "The Turbulent Moros," *Boston Evening Transcript*, July 13, 1903; "Treachery of a Moro," *New York Times*, May 27, 1902; "The Warlike Moros of Mindanao," *Argus*, May 21, 1904, 12.

16. "The Juramentado," *Mindanao Herald*, December 26, 1903, 2–3.

17. Buel, *Louisiana and the Fair*, 1713.

18. See, for example in the *Mindanao Herald*, "Ran Amuck in Jolo," January 21, 1905, 1; "Private Morse Stopped Him," April 29, 1905, 1; "His Head Was Hot," October 15, 1904, 1; "Moro Runs Amuck," December 19, 1903, 1; "American Soldier Ran Amuck," April 22, 1905, 1; "Why Moros Run Amuck," December 22, 1906, 1; "Filipino Runs Amuck," May 5, 1906, 3. See also "Topics of the Times," *New York Times*, December 10, 1903.

19. "A Descriptive Story of the Philippine Exhibit," *World's Fair Bulletin* 5, no. 8 (June 1904): 50.

20. *Report of the Philippine Exposition Board* (1905), 20, 228, 569.

21. J. C. Abel, "The Camera in Science, Art and Pastime," *Modern Culture* 12, no. 3 (November 1900): 201, 202, 203, 204.

22. For an informative discussion of photography and "Kodaking" at the St. Louis World's Fair, see Vergara, *Displaying Filipinos*; Max Quanchi, "Visual Histories and Photographic Evidence," *Journal of Pacific History* 41, no. 2 (September 2006): 165–73; Julie K. Brown, *Contesting Images: Photography and the World's Columbian Exposition* (Tucson: University of Arizona Press, 1994); Sarah Pink, Laszlo Kurti, and Ana Isabel Alfonso, eds., *Working Images: Visual Research and Representation in Ethnography* (New York: Routledge, 2004).

23. "Our World's Fair Wonderers," *Daily Journal* (Telluride), October 10, 1904, 4.

24. Corbey, "Ethnographic Showcases," 362.

25. Photo books containing exotic and voyeuristic images of the live exhibits were also sold ubiquitously throughout the fairgrounds. These books were advertised as indispensible souvenirs and proof of attendance. For a particularly elaborate photo book containing images from the Philippine Village, see C. S. Jackson et al., *Jackson's Famous Photographs of the Louisiana Purchase Exposition* (Chicago: Metropolitan Syndicate Press, 1904).

26. Clevenger, *"Indescribably Grand,"* 132.

27. Lowenstein, *Official Guide*, 118.

28. "Don't Photograph Savage Moros!" *St. Louis Republic*, May 10, 1904, 6.

29. "Insure Your Life before Photographing the Moros," *St. Louis Post-Dispatch*, May 15, 1904, A12B.

30. "Bolomen Rout Camera Fiend," *St. Louis Post-Dispatch*, May 6, 1904, 5.

31. Cohn, *Colonialism*, 10.

32. "War On! Moros Demand Salary," *St. Louis Post-Dispatch*, May 30, 1904, 6.

33. For a lively account of a violent encounter between a Moro sultan and an Igorrot chieftain, see "Brass Ring Parts Filipino Friends," *St. Louis Post-Dispatch*, October 15, 1904, 1.

34. Wax was unfortunately called away to Albany, New York, after the death of his mother. See "Fear Trouble among Moros," *St. Louis Republic*, May 14, 1904, 1.

35. This episode also played into long-standing colonial tropes of Oriental despotism, harking back to familiar notions of tyranny and kingship in the West. Consider the following from an article printed in the *Evening Star*: "Cruel as Apaches. As a rule the datto is a haughty, ignorant, and cruel savage, much more so than the chiefs of our North American Indian tribes. He is an absolute despot, exercising his own will and gratifying his passions and whims regardless of the lives and property of his subjects and turning them to his own account whenever he desires. His authority is supported by the panditas or Moslem priests, who teach the people that his person is divine, that he is the representative of Allah and that whoever raises his hand against him will suffer eternal torment. And so strong is the hold of the Moslem religion upon the people that, in spite of the injustice tyranny and cruelty of the dattos, there is not a single case of rebellion; no one can cite a single instance in which a slave or vassal has been insubordinate or has used violence against his datto." "Chiefs of the Moros," *Evening Star*, July 30, 1904, 8.

36. "Moro Politics Are Warming Up," *St. Louis Post-Dispatch*, August 23, 1904, 20.

37. Robert Moss, "The 1904 World's Fair: A Turning Point for American Food," January 11, 2016, http://www.seriouseats.com/2016/01/food-history-1904-worlds-fair-st-louis.html.

38. Upton Sinclair, *The Jungle* (New York: Dover Publications, 2001).

39. Kirshenblatt-Gimblett, "Objects of Ethnography," 409.

40. Benedict, *Anthropology of World's Fairs*, 44.

41. See, for a small sample, "Dog Feast to Be Reward of Igorrotes' Work," *St. Louis Republic*, May 8, 1904, 1; and in the *St. Louis Post-Dispatch*: "Letters from the People: Igorrote Dog Feasts," June 20, 1904, 6, "Letters from the People: Igorrote Cruelty Shocks a Child," June 29, 1904, 10, "At Last Igorrotes Have Dog Banquet," April 17, 1904, A5B, "Shan't Eat Fido if He Can Help It," April 5, 1904, 2, "Is It Beef, Trust, Speaking through Humane Society, That Would Rob Irrogote of His Cherished Dog Meat?" April 6, 1904, 9, "Igorrote Men Enjoy Dog Feast while Hungry Better Halves Look Enviously On," May 16, 1904, 12, "Oh, Say! But Won't This Be the Limit?" August 7, 1904, 6, "Well, Here I Am," March 31, 1904, 13, "This Is Last Day for Score of Dogs," May 15, 1904, 3B, "Igorrotes Attack the Disease Spirit," May 4, 1904, 9, "All Flesh Devourers," April 11, 1904, 4, "All Day Vigil to Protect Fido," April 11, 1904, 7, "Lion Tamer's Dog Rescued," June 13, 1904, 3, "Igorrote Feast Ordered," May 13, 1904, 7, "The Igorrote Dog Butchers," May 21, 1904, 4, "Igorrotes Vainly Chase Stray Dog," June 22, 1904, 16, "Tie Fido before Igorrotes Get Him," March 30, 1904, 1.

42. Kirshenblatt-Gimblett, "Objects of Ethnography," 409.

43. "Moro Cannibals Closely Guarded," *St. Louis Republic*, May 12, 1904, 8.

44. See, for example, "Our Cannibal Cousins," *Columbian* (Bloomsburg, PA), May 18, 1905, 7; "Eat Human Flesh," *Hartford Herald*, May 15, 1904; "Our Cannibal Cousins," *Reidsville Review*, September 20, 1904, 4.

45. "News of Slaughter Pleases Moros," *St. Louis Republic*, May 13, 1904, 1.

46. "Moro Cannibals Closely Guarded," *St. Louis Republic*, May 12, 1904, 8; article reprinted as "Our Cannibal Cousins," *Columbian* (Bloomsburg, PA), May 18, 1905, 7.

47. Breitbart, *A World on Display*, 38.

48. Crew and Sims, "Locating Authenticy," 163.

2. Nostalgia and the Familiar Savage

1. Rydell, *All the World's a Fair*, 155.

2. John Brisben Walker, "What the Louisiana Purchase Exposition Is," *Cosmopolitan* 38, no. 5 (September 1904): 600.

3. Buel, *Louisiana and the Fair*, 1697.

4. See Lears, *No Place of Grace*; Lears, "Salvation to Self-Realization"; Fritzsche, *Stranded in the Present*; Blix, "Charting the 'Transitional Period'"; Richard Hofstadter, *The Paranoid Style in American Politics*, 145–87; Bauman, *Modernity and Ambivalence*.

5. Frederick Jackson Turner's famous "frontier thesis" was originally articulated in his paper "The Significance of the Frontier in American History," which was presented at the American Historical Association meeting during the 1893 Chicago World's Fair. See the *Annual Report of the American Historical Association for the Year 1893*, in US Congressional Serial Set, No. 3170. For an expanded and more thorough discussion of his thesis, see Frederick Jackson Turner, *The Frontier in American History*. A useful look at Turner's "frontier thesis" in modern historiography can be found in Mary Ellen Jones, ed., *The American Frontier: Opposing Viewpoints* (San Diego: Greenhaven Press, 1994).

6. See Bederman, *Manliness and Civilization*; Hoganson, *Fighting for American Manhood*; and Mangan and Walvin, *Manliness and Morality*.

7. For a fascinating conversation on the perceived regenerating powers of violence, see Richard Slotkin, *Regeneration through Violence: The Mythology of the American Frontier, 1600–1860* (Norman: University of Oklahoma Press, 2000). See also Slotkin, *Gunfighter Nation: The Myth of the Frontier in Twentieth Century America* (Norman: University of Oklahoma Press, 1998); Slotkin, *The Fatal Environment: The Myth of the Frontier in the Age of Industrialization, 1800–1890* (Norman: University of Oklahoma Press, 1998). For an unsurpassed literary commentary on the subject, see Cormac McCarthy, *Blood Meridian: Or the Evening Redness in the West* (New York: Vintage, 1992).

8. Quoted in Francis, *Universal Exposition*, 146. Roosevelt's presidency during the formative years of American colonialism in the Philippines was highly appropriate, considering his embodiment of the philosophical principles and ideologies that undergirded the imperial project. Although articulated years before the American colonial occupation of the Philippines, his notions of masculinity and the American frontier character seemed especially applicable to Moro Province after the closing of the western American frontier. For the best example of these notions, see Roosevelt's four-volume work, *Winning of the West*, presidential ed. (Lincoln: University of Nebraska Press, 1995).

9. For an interesting discussion of manifestation of American masculinity in Moro Province, see Michael C. Hawkins, "Masculinity Reborn: Chivalry, Misogyny, Potency, and Violence in the Philippines' Muslim South, 1899–1914," *Journal of Southeast Asian Studies* 44, no. 2 (June 2013): 250–65; Hawkins, "Managing a Massacre: Savagery, Civility, and Gender in Moro Province in the Wake of Bud Dajo," *Philippine Studies* 58, no. 1 (2011): 81–103; Hawkins, "Frontier Justice, Colonial Justice, and the Spaces In Between in the Southern Philippines, 1898–1913," *Siliman Journal* 53, no. 1 (October 2012): 193–206.

10. See G. Stanley Hall, *Adolescence: Its Psychology and Its Relations to Physiology, Anthropology, Sociology, Sex, Crime, Religion, and Education*, vols. 1–2 (New York: D. Appleton, 1904). This work is also analyzed exceptionally well in Bederman's *Manliness and Civilization*.

11. Bass, "Jolo and the Moros," 1158ad–59ac.

12. *Census of the Philippines Islands* (1903), 1:564.

13. John Roberts White (a.k.a. Colonel John Roberts), *Bullets and Bolos: Fifteen Years in the Philippine Islands* (New York: Century, 1928), 194.

14. It should be noted that the Moros were also deeply imbued with these western frontier tropes. Even today one cannot help but notice hitching posts, building facades, and a pervasive affinity for single action revolvers and "outlaw" country music in certain areas of the Autonomous Region of Muslim Mindanao. Ron K. Edgerton insightfully explores the prevalence of the "American West" in Mindanao's popular culture in his article "Americans, Cowboys, and Cattlemen on the Mindanao Frontier," in *Reappraising an Empire: New Perspectives on Philippine-American History*, ed. Peter W. Stanley (Harvard University Press, 1984), 237–59.

15. *Souvenir of the Philippine Exposition*, 62.

16. Buel, *Louisiana and the Fair*, 1732.

17. See E. Taylor Atkins, *Primitive Selves: Koreana in the Japanese Colonial Gaze, 1910–1945* (Berkeley: University of California Press, 2010).

18. Zachman, "World's Fair Souvenirs," 207; Clevenger, "*Indescribably Grand*," 28–29.

19. Fabian, *Time and the Other*, 27, 88.

20. Walker, "What the Louisiana Purchase Exposition Is," 600. See also Fabian, *Time and the Other*, 75.

21. Fabian, *Time and the Other*, 11.

22. See Turner, *The Frontier in American History*, as well as his "frontier thesis," (1893).

23. "American Character and the Philippines," *Mindanao Herald*, August 12, 1905, 9–10.

24. *Souvenir of the Philippine Exposition*, 62.

25. "Malay Pirates at the Fair," *St. Louis Post-Dispatch*, May 15, 1904, C5.

26. Lowenstein, *Official Guide*, 118.

27. "Gay Pants a Fad among the Dudes of the Mandanaos," *St. Louis Post-Dispatch*, May 3, 1904, 11. Evander Berry Wall (1860–1940) was a high society gentleman of some note in the fashion world. A native New Yorker, Wall also lived for extended periods of time in Paris. After inheriting two million dollars in his early twenties, Wall became a regular patron of trendy restaurants, society functions, and elite vacation spots. He was known for his extravagant dress and was proclaimed "King of the Dudes" in 1883. By 1888 the title caught on among New York journalists, and caricatures of Wall frequently appeared in magazines and newspapers. See "With Well Dressed Men," *New York Times*, July 22, 1902; "King of the Dudes: A Bright Social Star's Temporary Eclipse. Mr. E. Berry Wall's Embarrassment—Some of the Incidents in a Very striking Career," *New York Times*, September 5, 1885.

28. "Moros Make Gums Glitter," *St. Louis Post-Dispatch*, September 21, 1904, 11.

29. Benedict, *Anthropology of World's Fairs*, 2.

30. Zachman, "World's Fair Souvenirs," 206; Gilbert, "World's Fairs," 23.

31. "Moros Refuse to 'Chow': Keep On Building Huts," *St. Louis Post-Dispatch*, May 5, 1904, 22.

32. *Census of the Philippine Islands* (1903), 2:566.

33. Ibid.

34. "The People of Mindanao and Jolo," *Mindanao Herald*, December 12, 1903, 5.

35. "The Gospel of Work," *Mindanao Herald*, August 12, 1905, 5.

36. "Editorial Comment," *Mindanao Herald*, June 10, 1905, 4.

37. "Our New Prosperity," *Daily Bulletin*, August 18, 1900, 3–4.

38. "Chinese Immigration," *Daily Bulletin*, February 15, 1903, 1; "The Hemp Industry," *Daily Bulletin*, 3; "Importation of Rice," *Daily Bulletin*, 16; "Filipino Labor," *Daily Bulletin*, September 17, 1903, 3.

39. "Pupils of 'Wild' School Don't Whisper or Throw Paper Wads," *St. Louis Post-Dispatch*, July 24, 1904, A5.

40. See Sarah Mondale, ed., *School: The Story of American Public Education* (New York: Beacon Press, 2002).

41. "This Filipino Hid $127 in Bamboo Tree," *St. Louis Post-Dispatch*, October 28, 1904, 15.

42. *Bulletin of the Bureau of Labor*, no. 65, July 1906 (Washington, DC: Government Printing Office, 1906), 54.

43. Francis, *Universal Exposition*, 189, vi.

44. Ibid., 55.

45. "The Workshop of the Modern Youngster," *Chicago Daily Tribune*, March 20, 1904, A2.

46. "Moro Boys Make Shoot-the-Chutes," *St. Louis Post-Dispatch*, August 23, 1904, 11; "In a Jiffy Filipinos Built a Shoot-the-Chutes," *St. Louis Post-Dispatch*, August 7, 1904, A3.

47. "Here's a Chance to Help Your Uncle Sam Assimilate Filipinos," *St. Louis Post-Dispatch*, November 17, 1904, 8. See also "Little Filipinos May Be Adopted," *St. Louis Republic*, November 16, 1904, 6.

48. See Michael Hawkins, *Making Moros: Imperial Historicism and American Military Rule in the Philippines' Muslim South* (DeKalb: Northern Illinois University Press, 2013), 55–56; Kramer, *Blood of Government*, 130–45.

49. Gonzalez, "Headhunter Itineraries," 150.

50. Mark Bennitt and Frank Parker Stockbridge, comps. and eds., *History of the Louisiana Purchase Exposition* (St. Louis: Universal Exposition Publishing, 1905), 718. See also Lowenstein, *Official Guide*, 37.

51. Parezo and Fowler, *Anthropology Goes to the Fair*, 255–56.

52. For the initial reaction, see "Conditions in Sulu Islands," *New York Times*, May 26, 1901, 5; "Plans for Abolishing Philippine Slavery," *New York Times*, December 21, 1901, 8; "America Abrogates Treaty with Moros," *New York Times*, March 15, 1904, 5; "Slavery in the Philippines," *Chicago Daily Tribune*, March 5, 1899, 50; Dean Worcester, *The Philippines Past and Present* (New York: Macmillan Press, 1914), 513. See also Michael Salman, *The Embarrassment of Slavery: Controversies over Bondage and Nationalism in the American Colonial Philippines* (Berkeley: University of California Press, 2001).

53. Bass, "Jolo and the Moros," 1158ad.

54. *RPC* (1901), vol. 3, quoted in "Plans for Abolishing Philippine Slavery," *New York Times*, December 21, 1901, 8.

55. *Census of the Philippine Islands* (1903), 2:570.

56. "The Moros," *Mindanao Herald*, March 19, 1904, 5.

57. "The History of Slavery and Emancipation," a speech delivered by H. T. Utley before the Democratic Association in Dubuque, Iowa, on February 12, 1863 (Philadelphia: John Campbell Publisher, 1863). See also James Hunt, *The Negro's Place in Nature: A Paper Read Before the London Anthropological Society* (New York: Van Evrie, Horton, 1866).

58. H. T. Utley, *The History of Slavery and Emancipation*, 7. For apologists, see R. W. Warren, *Nellie Norton: or Southern Slavery and the Bible* (Macon: Burke, Boykin, 1864); T. W. Hoit, *The Right of American Slavery* (St. Louis: L. Bushnell, 1860); C. Blancher Thompson, *The Nachash Origin of the Black and Mixed Races* (St. Louis: George Knapp, 1860); Thornton Stringfellow, *A Brief Examination of Scripture Testimony on the Institution of Slavery* (Washington, DC: Congressional Globe Office, 1850).

59. Arthur MacArthur, in *Affairs in the Philippine Islands. Hearings before the Committee on the Philippines of the United States Senate*, 57th Congress, 1st Sess., Doc. 331, Part 2 (Washington, DC: Government Printing Press, 1902), 1962.

60. Although varying in practice, slavery in the southern Philippines was often a horrific institution. See James Warren's prolific body of work including *The Sulu Zone: The World Capitalist Economy and the Historical Imagination* (Amsterdam: VU University Press, 1998); Warren, "Ransom, Escape and Debt Repayment in the Sulu Zone, 1750–1898," in *Bonded Labour and Debt in the Indian Ocean World*, ed. Alessandro Stanziani and Gwyn Campbell (London: Pickering and Chatto, 2013), 87–101; Warren, "The Port of Jolo: International Trade and Slave Raiding," in *Pirates, Ports, and Coasts in Asia: Historical and Contemporary Perspectives*, ed. John Kleinen and Manon Osseweijer (Singapore: Institute of Southeast Asian Studies, 2007), 178–99; Warren, "The Iranun and Balangingi Slaving Voyage: Middle Passages in the Sulu Zone," in *Many Middle Passages*, ed. Marcus Rediker, Emma Christopher,

Cassandra Pybus (Berkeley: University of California Press, 2007), 52–71; Warren, "Saltwater Slavers and Captives in the Sulu Zone, 1768–1878," *Slavery and Abolition: A Journal of Slave and Post-slave Studies* 31, no. 3 (2010): 429–49; Warren, "The Structure of Slavery in the Sulu Zone in the Late Eighteenth and Nineteenth Centuries," *Slavery and Abolition: A Journal of Slave and Post-slave Studies* 24 (2010): 111–28; Warren, "Slave Markets and Exchange in the Malay World: The Sulu Sultanate, 1770–1878," *Journal of Southeast Asian Studies* 8, no. 2 (1977): 162–75. See also Hawkins, "Frontier Justice."

61. "Human Beings in Slavery at World's Fair," *St. Louis Post-Dispatch*, May 4, 1904, 1.

62. "Slaves at St. Louis Fair," *New York Times*, May 5, 1904, 3.

63. Robert J. C. Young, *Colonial Desire: Hybridity in Theory, Culture, and Race* (New York: Routledge, 1995), 97. For recent scholarship see, for example, Victor Roman Mendoza, *Metroimperial Intimacies: Fantasy, Racial-Sexual Governance, and the Philippines in U.S. Imperialism, 1899–1913* (Durham: Duke University Press, 2015); Bederman, *Manliness and Civilization*; Hoganson, *Fighting for American Manhood*; Paul Lyons, *American Pacifism: American Explorations of the Colonialism, Race, Gender and Sexuality* (New York: Routledge, 2005); Stoler, *Carnal Knowledge and Imperial Power*; Donald J. Mrozek, "The Habit of Victory: The American Military and the Cult of Manliness," in Mangan and Walvin, *Manliness and Morality*, 220–41; Hawkins, "Managing a Massacre"; Hawkins, "Masculinity Reborn."

64. See *RPC* (1900), 3:376. This was likely a misinterpretation of Moro dowry arrangements, however.

65. Census of the Philippine Islands (1903), 2:565.

66. *RPC* (1904), pt. 1, 9.

67. *RPC* (1901), 3:372.

68. Census of the Philippine Islands (1903), 2:563–64.

69. Ibid., 572.

70. See David Brody, *Visualizing American Empire: Orientalism and Imperialism in the Philippines* (Chicago: University of Chicago Press, 2010); Warwick Anderson, *Colonial Pathologies: American Tropical Medicine, Race, and Hygiene in the Philippines* (Durham: Duke University Press, 2006); Anderson, "The Trespass Speaks: White Masculinity and Colonial Breakdown," *American Historical Review* 102, no. 5 (December 1997): 1343–70.

71. Kirshenblatt-Gimblett, "Objects of Ethnography," 398.

72. Charles M. Kurtz, *The St. Louis World's Fair of 1904* (St. Louis: Gottschalk, 1903), 113.

73. Lawrence L. Samuel, *The End of Innocence: The 1964–1965 New York World's Fair* (Syracuse: Syracuse University Press, 2007), 20.

74. Kurtz, *St. Louis World's Fair*, 113.

75. Aram A. Yengoyan, "Culture, Ideology and World's Fairs: Colonizer and Colonized in Comparative Perspectives," in Rydell and Gwinn, *Fair Representations*, 70. It should be noted that there were many positive views of Islam as well, particularly among bourgeois American elites. Timony Marr, for example, examines the popular, socially minded uses of Islamic civilization among American progressives, particularly abolitionists and members of the temperance movement in the nineteenth century. See Timothy Marr, *The Cultural Roots of American Islamicism* (Cambridge: Cambridge University Press, 2006).

76. The 1903 census, for example, took great care in describing the Moros' "physical characteristics" including "complexion," "hair," and physical build. "They are somewhat taller than the average Filipino," recorded the census, "straight and well formed, and often strong and stockily built, with well-developed calves." Census of the Philippine Islands (1903), 1:563. See also *RPC* (1903), pt. 1, 81; *RPC* (1901), 3:371; Hugh L. Scott, *Some Memories of a Soldier* (New York: Century, 1928), 312, 283; Colonel Owen J. Sweet, "The Moro, the Fighting-Man of the Philippines," *Harper's Weekly*, June 9, 1906, 0808d.

77. Bederman, *Manliness and Civilization*; see also Hawkins, "Masculinity Reborn."

78. For an excellent discussion of overcivilization, waning masculinity, the role of frontiers, and the formation of an American character, see Frederick Jackson Turner's famous "frontier thesis," originally articulated in his paper "The Significance of the Frontier in American History," presented at the American Historical Association meeting during the 1893 Chicago World's Fair, and found in *Annual Report of the American Historical Association for the Year 1893*, in US Congressional Serial Set, No. 3170. For an expanded and more thorough discussion of his thesis, see Turner, *The Frontier in American History*. A useful look at Turner's "frontier thesis" in modern historiography can be found in Jones, *The American Frontier*. Theodore Roosevelt's advocacy of the "strenuous life" is also instructive, perhaps best embodied in his work *Winning of the West*. Particularly pertinent on this point were G. Stanley Hall's theories of racial "recapitulation" and declining American masculinity (discussed earlier). Concerned with the emasculating effects of modernity on young boys, Hall advocated maintaining the Darwinistic struggle for racial supremacy by exposing young men to savagery, in order to hone their competitive skills. By maintaining a visceral connection with primitive man (known as racial recapitulation), Hall believed that young American men would not lose their competitive edge and succumb to racial suicide. See Hall, *Adolescence*. Additionally, discussion of modern anxieties and the American quest for authentic experience is treated exceptionally well in Lears, *No Place of Grace*; Lears, "From Salvation to Self-Realization"; and Bederman, *Manliness and Civilization*.

79. "Killed Fourteen Men to Secure His Wife," *St. Louis Republic*, May 15, 1904, 4.

80. The regenerative powers of frontier violence have been a topic of much discussion in scholarly work and literature. Perhaps the best on the subject are Slotkin, *Regeneration through Violence*; Slotkin, *Gunfighter Nation*; Slotkin, *The Fatal Environment*. See also Cormac McCarthy's novel *Blood Meridian*.

81. "Wanted—Six Wives for Moro Sultan," *St. Louis Post-Dispatch*, September 6, 1904, 20.

82. Perhaps the most famous historical practice of polygamy in the United States was by Latter-Day Saints, also known as Mormons. Mormons first taught plural marriages in the 1830s, began to enter into plural marriages by the 1840s, and formally defended the practice in the 1850s. It immediately provoked national outrage and intense persecution. In 1856 the Republican Party platform took direct aim at Mormon polygamy, declaring it one of the "twin relics of barbarism" along with slavery. In 1857 James Buchannan dispatched twenty-five hundred federal troops to Utah to unseat Governor Brigham Young, precipitating the Utah War. This action was quickly followed by a series of congressional acts, including the Morrill Anti-Bigamy Act (1862), the Edmunds Act (1882), and the Edmunds-Tucker Act (1887), designed to punish the practice. Mormons formally ended plural marriage by declaration in 1890. President of the church, Joseph F. Smith, formally disavowed polygamy before Congress in 1904, the same year as the World's Fair. It is interesting to note that the most intense persecutions against Mormons occurred in Missouri, where Latter-Day Saints were driven from their lands by the infamous "Extermination Order" (Missouri Executive Order 44) issued by Governor Lilburn Boggs. See *Republican Party Platform of 1856*, June 18, 1856; Cardell K. Jacobson and Lara Burton, eds., *Modern Polygamy in the United States: Historical, Cultural and Legal Issues* (New York: Oxford University Press, 2011); B. H. Roberts, *Comprehensive History of the Church of Jesus Christ of Latter-Day Saints*, vol. 1 (Salt Lake City: Deseret News Press, 1930); William G. Hartley, "Missouri's 1838 Extermination Order and the Mormon's Forced Removal to Illinois," *Mormon Historical Studies* 2, no. 1 (2001): 5–27; Richard Bushman, *Joseph Smith: A Rough Stone Rolling* (New York: Vintage Books, 2007); John Cook Bennett, *The History of the Saints; Or, An Expose of Joseph Smith and Mormonism* (Boston: Leland and Whiting, 1842).

83. "Philippine Exhibit," *World's Fair Bulletin* 4, no. 12 (October 1903): 7; *Report of the Philippine Exposition Board* (1905), 154.

84. "American Chosen as a Moro Sultan," *St. Louis Post-Dispatch*, June 12, 1904, B5.

85. Although in the minority, there were dissenting voices regarding the perceived dangerous effects of proximity to native bodies and culture on the health of white Americans. A former teacher in Manila, for example, wrote a scathing anonymous editorial in the *St. Louis Post-Dispatch*. He or she wrote: "Did the Spaniards improve themselves by mingling with the Filipinos? Not at all. They degraded themselves. The white man is a fool for bearing what has been termed by Mr. Kipling 'The White Man's burden,' and the sooner we free the Filipinos and let them work out their own salvation the better for us . . . the Filipinos are in a tropical climate and consequently are less vigorous than the Japanese. . . . The white man or the white woman who stays in the islands for any length of time, in the language of the soldier boys, goes buggy." See "Is Educating the Filipinos a Mistake?," *St. Louis Post-Dispatch*, August 26, 1904, 6.

86. "American Chosen as a Moro Sultan," *St. Louis Post-Dispatch*, June 12, 1904, B5.

87. Brody, *Visualizing American Empire*, 3.

3. Measuring Moros

1. Michel Foucault, *The History of Sexuality, Vol. 1: An Introduction* (New York: Vintage Books, 1978); Thomas Laqueur, *Making Sex: Body and Gender from the Greeks to Freud* (Cambridge, MA: Harvard University Press, 1992); Nicolas Bancel et al., eds., *The Invention of Race: Scientific and Popular Representations* (New York: Routledge, 2014); Thomas C. Holt, "Marking: Race, Race-Making, and the Writing of History," *American Historical Review* 100, no. 10 (February 1995): 1–20.

2. Kramer, *Blood of Government*, 2.

3. Elizabeth M. Collingham, *Imperial Bodies: The Physical Experience of the Raj, c. 1800–1947* (Cambridge, MA: Polity Press, 2001).

4. See, for example, Pat Shipman, *The Evolution of Racism* (Cambridge, MA: Harvard University Press, 1994).

5. Susan Brownell, "Introduction," in *The Anthropology Days and Olympic Games: Sport, Race, and American Imperialism*, ed. Susan Brownell (Lincoln: University of Nebraska Press, 2008), 14–15. See also McGee, "The Trend of Human Progress."

6. Gonzalez, "Headhunter Itineraries," 152.

7. Francis, *Universal Exposition*, 525.

8. *RPC* (1901), 3:331.

9. Buel, *Louisiana and the Fair*, 1709.

10. Bill Ashcroft, Gareth Griffiths, and Helen Tiffin, eds., *Postcolonial Studies: The Key Concepts* (New York: Routledge, 2013), 21. See also Dorian Bell, "Cavemen among Us: Genealogies of Atavism from Zola's *La Bête Humaine* to Chabrol's *Le Boucher*," *French Studies: A Quarterly Review* 62, no. 1 (January 2008): 39–52; Andrea Cabajsky, "Catholic Gothic: Atavism, Orientalism, and Genetic Change in Charles De Guise's *Le Capau Diable*," in *Unsettled Remains: Canadian Literature and Postcolonial Gothic*, ed. Cynthia Sugars and Gerry Turcotte (Ontario: Wilfrid Laurier University, 2009), 1–29.

11. Bennett, *Birth of the Museum*, 192.

12. Lowenstein, *Official Guide*, 93.

13. McGee, "Anthropology," 4.

14. Nancy J. Parezo, "A 'Special Olympics,'" in Brownell, *The 1904 Anthropology Days*, 71.

15. Ibid., 71–72.

16. McGee, "Anthropology," 8–9.

17. Breitbart, *A World on Display*, 18; Jose D. Fermin, *1904 World's Fair: The Filipino Experience* (Quezon City: University of the Philippines Press, 2004), 156.

18. Brownell, "Introduction," 34.

19. "Features of the World's Fair," *St. Louis Republic*, May 26, 1904, 1.

20. "Anthropological: Concerning the Early Beginnings of Men and Women," *Cosmopolitan* 38, no. 5 (September 1904): 609–10.

21. Parezo, "Special Olympics," 72.

22. For example, Filipinos comprised 137 of 224 indigenous people subjected to Bruner's study on "The Hearing of Primitive Peoples." Ratios were similar in other experiments. See Frank G. Bruner, "The Hearing of Primitive Peoples," *Archives of Psychology* 2, no. 11 (1908): 1–113.

23. "To Measure Men of All Nations," *St. Louis Republic*, May 1, 1904, 9.

24. The word *bughaw* was frequently used by both Tagalog and Visayan speakers in much the same way that "blue" was and is used by English speakers; most commonly to describe the color of the sky or the eye color of foreigners, for example. Modern usage has largely replaced *bughaw* with the Spanish derived *asul*, but *bughaw* still finds its way into usage, and it was commonly known by Filipinos in 1904. See, for example, Leo James English, *English-Tagalog Dictionary* (Quezon City: Kalayaan Press, 1977), 105.

25. Fermin, *1904 World's Fair*, 156. Bruner, however, did claim to find racial disparities in hearing, which he later published. Bruner, "The Hearing of Primitive Peoples," 113.

26. Robert E. MacLaury, "Linguistic Relativity and the Plasticity of Categorization: Universalism in a New Key," in *Explorations in Linguistic Relativity*, ed. Martin Putz and Jarjolijn H. Verspoor (Amsterdam: John Benjamins, 2000), 252.

27. See Lee D. Baker, *From Savage to Negro: Anthropology and the Construction of Race, 1896–1954* (Berkeley: University of California Press, 1998), 68–69.

28. Woodworth quoted in Hans J. Massaquoi, "Lefties—A Maligned Minority," *Ebony* 22, no. 7 (May 1967): 68.

29. W. J. McGee, "Anthropology at the Louisiana Purchase Exposition," *Science*, n.s., vol. 22, no. 573 (December 22, 1905): 816, 821.

30. See, for example, Hawkins, "Undecided Empire."

31. See, for example, in the *St. Louis Post-Dispatch*, "Philippine Soldier and His Bride Saw Each Other First Time at Wedding," April 3, 1904, 2B; "A Madame Butterfly of the Philippines," June 14, 1903, B7; "Filipino Wife Can't Protest," November 20, 1903, 8; "Filipino Wife Worries Him," May 23, 1903, 10; "Burbank's Filipino Wife, Far from Being Savage, Is Educated, Woman of Splendid Family," October 22, 1905, 11; "Will Try Burbank," September 20, 1905, 16; "Court of Officers Cashiers Mullikin," January 22, 1905, A6; "Filipino Wives Appeal to Justice," March 6, 1904, A8B; "Filipino Wives Are Permanent," May 21, 1903, 6. See also "Says Spouse Met Soldier at Dance," *St. Louis Republic*, November 3, 1905, 14.

32. For the controversy, in the *St. Louis Post-Dispatch*, see "Police Separate Filipinos and White Women," July 17, 1904, A8; "Scouts Lose First Battle with Marines," July 7, 1904, 1; "St. Louis Color Line Problem at the Fair," July 3, 1904, B3; "Marines Threaten Flirting Scouts," July 6, 1904, 9; "Wound Received in Café Affray Fatal," November 4, 1904, 4; "Girl and Filipino Escort Hissed Out," November 7, 1904, 1; "White Man Is Fatally Stabbed by Filipinos," July 24, 1904, A1; "Man and Woman Shoot Each Other," October 2, 1904, A1. See also Kramer, *Blood of Government*, 260–79. For defense, in the *St. Louis Post-Dispatch*, see "Who Could Blame Flirting Scouts?" July 14, 1904, 11; "Filipino Officer Defends Soldiers," July 28, 1904, 11; "A Polite Filipino," June 23, 1904, 12. See also "Philippine Scouts Arouse Admiration," *St. Louis Republic*, April 16, 1904, 8.

33. "Here's a Chance to Help Your Uncle Sam Assimilate Filipinos," *St. Louis Post-Dispatch*, November 17, 1904, 8; "Little Filipinos May be Adopted," *St. Louis Republic*, November 16, 1904, 6.

34. "Malay Pirates at the Fair," *St. Louis Post-Dispatch*, May 15, 1904, C5.

35. *The Official Handbook of the Philippines*, pt. 1, p. 161.

36. Buel, *Louisiana and the Fair*, 1738–39; Lowenstein, *Official Guide*, 110; "The Government Philippine Exposition," *Scientific American* 91, no. 4 (July 23, 1904): 66.

37. *Census of the Philippine Islands* (1903), 1:563.

38. Mark Dyreson, *Making the American Team: Sport, Culture, and the Olympic Experience* (Champaign: University of Illinois Press, 1997), 80.

39. Francis, *Universal Exposition*, 50–51, 55.

40. "The Olympic Games," *World's Fair Bulletin* 5, no. 12 (October 1904): 16.

41. Kurtz, *Saint Louis World's Fair*, 76.

42. Dyreson, *Making the American Team*, 82.

43. Francis, *Universal Exposition*, 536.

44. "The Olympic Games," *World's Fair Bulletin* 5, no. 12 (October 1904): 16.

45. Dyreson, *Making the American Team*, 82.

46. In 1899 McGee wrote: "While American athletes defeat the descendants of gladiators on their own ground; the average Briton or American is too big for the armor of the mail-clad hero of medieval history; the rough-riding scion of enlightenment appals by his superior stature the puny soldiery of unprogressive monarchism; it is a poor modern year that does not mark the breaking of one or more world-records in athletics. . . . [V]iewing the human world as it is, white and strong are synonymous terms." McGee, "The Trend of Human Progress," 413, 446.

47. *RPC* (1901), 3:371.

48. Bass, "Jolo and the Moros," 1158ad.

49. Sweet, "The Moro," 808d.

50. Scott, *Some Memories*, 316.

51. "Malay Pirates at the Fair," *St. Louis Post-Dispatch*, May 15, 1904, C5.

52. "Filipinos of Four Tribes Play Odd Native Games with Great Skill and Agility," *St. Louis Post-Dispatch*, July 17, 1904, 4.

53. James E. Sullivan, *Spalding's Official Athletic Almanac for 1905* (New York: American, 1905), 249.

54. W. J. McGee to William P. Wilson, June 13, 1904, quoted in Parezo, "Special Olympics," 85.

55. McGee to Wilson, June 28, 1904, quoted in Parezo, "Special Olympics," 86.

56. "Partial List of Native Participants in Anthropology Days," quoted in Parezo, "Special Olympics," 88.

57. The events were the 100-yard dash, 100-meter dash, 440-yard dash, 120-yard hurdles, 1-mile run, running broad jump, shot put, baseball throw for distance, baseball throw for accuracy, weight throwing, running high jump, archery, tug-of-war, pole climbing 50 feet, bola throw, and javelin throw.

58. Parezo, "Special Olympics," 92–93.

59. "A Novel Athletic Contest," *World's Fair Bulletin* 5, no. 11 (September 1904): 50.

60. Sullivan, *Spalding's Official Athletic Almanac*, 249, 259.

61. Parezo, "Special Olympics," 96.

62. Brownell, "Introduction," 6.

63. Parezo, "Special Olympics," 106. In his retrospective account of the fair, Francis attempted to put a positive spin on Anthropology Days by touting its scientific value: "Perhaps the most notable special events participated in by the primitive tribes present at the

Exposition were the Athletic competitions conducted under the direction of James E. Sullivan, the chief of the department of Physical Culture, on August 12 and 13, which were known as Anthropology Days, at the Stadium. In these extraordinary competitions practically every alien race represented upon the exposition grounds participated. The events were carefully arranged and faithfully carried out to demonstrate the comparative skill, speed and endurance capacity of the contesting peoples; also to establish their comparative efficiency in these attributes in relation to the civilized races. The records secured as a result of these contests are of distinct scientific value, and have been carefully compiled and preserved." Francis, *Universal Exposition*, 230.

64. "A Novel Athletic Contest," *World's Fair Bulletin* 5, no. 11 (September 1904): 50.

65. Sullivan, *Spalding's Official Athletic Almanac*, 251–53, 255, 258–59.

66. Parezo, "Special Olympics," 104.

67. "Pygmies Outdo Savage Athletes," *St. Louis Post-Dispatch*, August 14, 1904, 7B.

68. "Peace 'twixt Moros and the Igorrotes," *St. Louis Post-Dispatch*, September 6, 1904, 5.

69. Parezo, "Special Olympics," 105.

70. Events included 100-yard dash, 120-yard hurdles, shot put, archery, standing broad jump, running high jump, spear throw, tree climbing, and the running broad jump.

71. "Moros First in Tribal Contests," *St. Louis Post-Dispatch*, September 16, 1904, 15.

72. "Moros Win the Honors in Intertribal Meet," *St. Louis Republic*, September 16, 1904, 2.

73. Francis, *Universal Exposition*, 230.

74. Fabian, *Time and the Other*, 153.

75. McGee, "Anthropology at the Louisiana Purchase Exposition," 815–16.

Conclusion

1. Breitbart, *World on Display*, 51.

2. Puerto Rico received only five thousand dollars for its display. Guam and Hawaii received nothing, though Hawaii initially benefited from an illegal fifty-thousand-dollar appropriation, which was quickly rescinded. See Fermin, *1904 World's Fair*, 39.

3. Kramer, "Making Concessions," 78, 80, 107.

4. Ibid., 78.

5. See *The Official Souvenir Program of the Philippines Carnival, February 27–March 3, 1908* (American Historical Collection, Rizal Library, Ateneo de Manila University, Philippines); "Don't Want Moros at Carnival," *Mindanao Herald*, January 18, 1908, 4; "A Continual Round of Pleasure," *Mindanao Herald*, January 4, 1908, 2; "Preparations for the Carnival," *Mindanao Herald*, January 18, 1908, 5; *Philippine Carnival*, Official Handbook, Manila, February 2–9, 1909 (American Historical Collection, Rizal Library, Ateneo de Manila University, Philippines), 1; "Carnival Exhibit of Moro Province," *Mindanao Herald*, January 16, 1909, 1; "Moro Invasion," *Manila Times*, January 28, 1909, in *50 Years with the Times*, pt. 1, January 1–June 30, 1909, 7; "Bayanihan: Moro Style," *Manila Times*, January 31, 1909, in *50 Years with the Times*, pt. 1, January 1–June 30, 1909, 83; "Plans for Arrival of Moro Delegation in Manila," *Mindanao Herald*, January 23, 1909, 1; "Moro Invasion," *Manila Times*, January 28, 1909, in *50 Years with the Times*, pt. 1, January 1–June 30, 1909, 74; "Carnival Day," *Manila Times*, February 2, 1909, in *50 Years with the Times*, pt. 1, January 1–June 30, 1909, 88; "Our Mohammedan Soldiers," *Philippine Monthly* 1, no. 12 (October 1910): 38–39. See also Hawkins, *Making Moros*, 48–53.

6. *Report of the Philippine Exposition Board* (1905), 27–29.

7. Ibid., 27–29, 48, 53.

8. "The Jurors of Awards, Philippine Section," *World's Fair Bulletin* 5, no. 12 (October 1904): 28; "Philippine Awards," *World's Fair Bulletin* 6, no. 1 (November 1904): 20; *Report of the Philippine Exposition Board* (1905), 40.

9. *Report of the Philippine Exposition Board* (1905), 63.

10. There were some dissenting voices from this view. For example, an anonymous editorial in the *Mindanao Herald* expressed disappointment with the display: "The Philippine exhibit at St. Louis has proved something of a disappointment, so far as being a benefit to the Islands is concerned. Several things have contributed to this state of affairs. First, our exhibit was too far removed from the main grounds and buildings[;] second, the character of exploitation given the Philippines was principally in the interests of the naked, dog-eating Igorrotes, which attracted the attention only of the morbidly curious; third, no one was employed to direct the attention of those who, by chance, did find their way into our grounds to the many valuable exhibits to be found on every hand. The attendance at the Philippine grounds at no time since the opening has exceeded 10 percent of the total attendance at the . . . fair grounds. Considered as a whole, Philippine participation at the Louisiana Purchase Exposition has been [a] very costly and unsatisfactory experiment." Untitled editorial, *Mindanao Herald*, October 15, 1904, 4. Much of this disappointment, however, can be contextualized within a subtle rivalry between Moro Province and Mountain Province, which were both key features of the "non-civilized" sectors of the colony. Take, for example, the following editorial published a few months previous in the same newspaper: "We are in receipt of vol.1, 'The Bontoc Igorot," published by the Ethnological Survey, doubtless at the expense of many thousands of dollars, the expenditure of which would have been infinitely more beneficial to the dog-eating head-hunters had it been expended in opening up and developing their section of the country. Perhaps such stuff as that being dished up by the Ethnological Survey has its place in the world, but it should be the result of collegiate rather than governmental research. If the people who pay for such useless and expensive appendages as the Ethnological Survey had any influence with their masters, the superimposed governors, that bureau would be traded off for a 'yaller' dog and the dog instantly shot." See "Editorial Comment," *Mindanao Herald*, June 10, 1905, 4.

11. *RPC* (1905), pt. 1, 345.

12. "Younger Igorrotes Want to Stay Here," *St. Louis Republic*, October 27, 1904, 6.

13. "Moros to Make Request of the President," *St. Louis Republic*, November 26, 1904, 2.

14. "At the Philippines," *World's Fair Bulletin* 6, no. 2 (December 1904): 3; "President at Fair Spends Busy Day," *New York Times*, November 27, 1904, 1; "President Greatly Pleased with Philippine Exhibit," *St. Louis Republic*, November 27, 1904, 5.

15. "Will Ask Court to Let Filipinos Stay," *St. Louis Post-Dispatch*, November 30, 1904, 1.

16. "Police Search for Two Moros," *St. Louis Republic*, December 4, 1904, 1; "Roll Call Shows One Moro Missing," *St. Louis Republic*, December 8, 1904, 7.

17. "Moro Too Hungry to Discriminate," *St. Louis Republic*, December 9, 1904, 9; "Filipinos Depart for Islands To-Day," *St. Louis Republic*, December 7, 1904, 8.

18. Francis, *Universal Exposition*, 201.

19. McGee, "The Trend of Human Progress," 447.

20. Buel, *Louisiana and the Fair*, 1971–72.

21. Breitbart, *A World on Display*, 46–47.

22. Corbey, "Ethnographic Showcases," 360.

23. Matt Bokovoy, "Review of *Anthropology Goes to the Fair: The 1904 Louisiana Purchase Exposition*," *Pacific Historical Review* 78, no. 2 (May 2009): 285.

24. Schrecker, *The Chinese Revolution*, 100.

25. Breitbart, *A World on Display*, 18.

26. Ibid.

27. Vergara, *Displaying Filipinos*, 145.

28. Marshall Berman, *All That Is Solid Melts into Air: The Experience of Modernity* (New York: Penguin Books, 1988). See also Karl Marx and Frederick Engels, *The Communist Manifesto* (New York: International Publishers, 2014).

29. Gilbert, "World's Fairs," 23.

30. Vergara, *Displaying Filipinos*, 144.

31. "Talks of Moros and Bagobas," *St. Louis Republic*, September 17, 1904, 1.

32. See, for example, "Starr Admires Model Moro," *Chicago Daily Tribune*, November 30, 1908, 4.

33. "Dim Prospects for Moros and Negritos," *St. Louis Republic*, November 16, 1904, 7.

34. F. H. Heinemann, "Reply to Historicism," *Philosophy* 21, no. 80 (November 1946): 251.

35. Fritzsche, *Stranded in the Present*, 4.

36. Michel Foucault, "Of Other Spaces," *Diacritics* 16 (Spring 1986): 26, quoted in Bennett, *Birth of the Museum*, 1.

37. David P. Barrows, *A History of the Philippines* (New York: American Book Company, 1905), 10.

38. Chakrabarty, *Provincializing Europe*, 87.

Epilogue

1. Anglo-Americans certainly do re-create their cultural past and heritage at a nearly constant rate. From Civil War reenactors to pioneer treks, from colonial pageants to Renaissance Fairs, Anglo-Americans demonstrate a persistent obsession with preserving the past through cultural display. However, these events are typically performed in the United States and are largely observed by American tourists.

2. Francis, *Universal Exposition*, vi.

3. "Polynesian Cultural Center to Launch Million Visitor per Year Strategic Initiative," *Business Wire*, April 27, 2017, https://businesswire.com/news/home/20170427006333/en/Polynesian-Cultural-Center-Launch-Million-Visitor-Year. Polynesian Cultural Center home site available from https://www.polynesia.com/villages/#.WoHJ9ZM-d-U.

4. *War Department Annual Reports, 1908*, vol. 7, pt. 1 (Washington, DC: Government Printing Office, 1909), 176.

5. See Vergara, *Displaying Filipinos*, 122–23; Fermin, *1904 World's Fair*, 192–93.

6. "Filipinos Are Preposterously Misrepresented," *St. Louis Post-Dispatch*, July 19, 1904, 1.

7. Kramer, *Blood of Government*, 73.

8. William Peterson, *Places for Happiness: Community, Self, and Performance in the Philippines* (Honolulu: University of Hawaii Press, 2016).

Bibliography

Newspapers and Journals

Argus
Boston Evening Transcript
Bulletin of the Bureau of Labor
Chicago Daily Tribune
Chicago Tribune
Clinton Morning Age
Columbian (Bloomsburg, PA)
Cosmopolitan
Daily Bulletin (Manila)
Daily Journal (Telluride)
Deseret News
Evening News (San Jose, CA)
Evening Star
Harper's Weekly
Hartford Herald

Mindanao Herald
National Tribune
New York Times
Omaha World Herald
Philippine Monthly
Reidsville Review
Spokane Daily Chronicle
St. Louis Post-Dispatch
St. Louis Republic
World's Fair Bulletin

Books and Articles

Abel, J. C. "The Camera in Science, Art and Pastime." *Modern Culture* 12, no. 3 (November 1900): 201–4.

Abinales, Patricio N. *Images of State Power: Essays on Philippine Politics from the Margins*. Quezon City: University of the Philippines Press, 1998.

———. *Making Mindanao: Cotabato and Davao in the Formation of the Philippine Nation-State*. Manila: Ateneo de Manila University Press, 2000.

ACT No. 514, Creating the Exposition Board. Circular Letter of Governor Taft and Information and Instructions for the Preparation for the Philippine Exhibit for the Louisiana Purchase Exposition to Be Held at St. Louis, Mo., USA, 1904. Manila: Bureau of Public Printing, 1902.

Affairs in the Philippine Islands. Hearings before the Committee on the Philippines of the United States Senate. 57th Cong., 1st Sess., Doc. 331, Part 2. Washington, DC: Government Printing Press, 1902.

Anderson, Benedict. *The Spectre of Comparisons: Nationalism, Southeast Asia and the World*. London: Verso, 1998.

Anderson, Warwick. *Colonial Pathologies: American Tropical Medicine, Race, and Hygiene in the Philippines*. Durham: Duke University Press, 2006.

———. "The Trespass Speaks: White Masculinity and Colonial Breakdown." *American Historical Review* 102, no. 5 (December 1997): 1343–70.

Ashcroft, Bill, Gareth Griffiths, and Helen Tiffin, eds. *Postcolonial Studies: The Key Concepts*. New York: Routledge, 2013.

Atkins, E. Taylor. *Primitive Selves: Koreana in the Japanese Colonial Gaze, 1910–1945*. Berkeley: University of California Press, 2010.

Baker, Lee D. *From Savage to Negro: Anthropology and the Construction of Race, 1896–1954*. Berkeley: University of California Press, 1998.

Bancel, Nicolas, Thomas, David, and Thomas, Dominic. *The Invention of Race: Scientific and Popular Representations*. New York: Routledge, 2014.

Barrows, David P. *A History of the Philippines*. New York: American Book Company, 1905.

Bass, John F. "Jolo and the Moros." *Harper's Weekly*, November 18, 1899, 1158ad–59ac.

Bauman, Zygmunt. *Modernity and Ambivalence*. Ithaca: Cornell University Press, 1991.

Bederman, Gail. *Manliness and Civilization: A Cultural History of Gender and Race in the United States, 1880–1917*. Chicago: University of Chicago Press, 1995.

Bell, Dorian. "Cavemen among Us: Genealogies of Atavism from Zola's *La Bête Humaine* to Chabrol's *Le Boucher*." *French Studies: A Quarterly Review* 62, no. 1 (January 2008): 39–52.

Benedict, Burton. *The Anthropology of World's Fairs: San Francisco's Panama Pacific International Exposition of 1915*. London: Lowie Museum of Anthropology, 1983.

Bennett, John Cook. *The History of the Saints; Or, An Expose of Joseph Smith and Mormonism*. Boston: Leland and Whiting, 1842.

Bennett, Tony. *The Birth of the Museum: History, Theory, Politics*. London: Routledge, 1995.

———. "The Exhibitionary Complex." *New Formations* 4 (Spring 1988): 73–102.

Bennitt, Mark, and Frank Parker Stockbridge, comps. and eds. *History of the Louisiana Purchase Exposition*. St. Louis: Universal Exposition Publishing Company, 1905.

Berman, Marshall. *All That Is Solid Melts into Air: The Experience of Modernity*. New York: Penguin Books, 1988.

Bhabha, Homi K. "Of Mimicry and Man: The Ambivalence of Colonial Discourse." In *Tensions of Empire: Colonial Cultures in a Bourgeois World*, edited by Frederick Cooper and Ann Laura Stoler, 152–60. Berkeley: University of California Press, 1997.

———. "Signs Taken for Wonders: Questions of Ambivalence and Authority under a Tree outside Delhi, May 1817." *Critical Inquiry* 12, no. 1 (Autumn 1985): 144–65.

Blix, Goran. "Charting the 'Transitional Period': The Emergence of Modern Time in the Nineteenth Century." *History and Theory* 45 (February 2006): 51–71.

Bogdan, Robert. *Freak Show: Presenting Human Oddities for Amusement and Profit*. Chicago: University of Chicago Press, 1988.

Bokovoy, Matt. "Review of *Anthropology Goes to the Fair: The 1904 Louisiana Purchase Exposition*." *Pacific Historical Review* 78, no. 2 (May 2009): 285.

Breitbart, Eric. *The World on Display: Photographs from the St. Louis World's Fair, 1904*. Albuquerque: University of New Mexico Press, 1997.

Brinton, Daniel G. "Professor Blumentritt's Studies of the Philippines." *American Anthropologist*, n.s., vol. 1, no. 1 (January 1899): 122–25.

Brody, David. *Visualizing American Empire: Orientalism and Imperialism in the Philippines*. Chicago: University of Chicago Press, 2010.

Brown, Julie K. *Contesting Images: Photography and the World's Columbian Exposition*. Tucson: University of Arizona Press, 1994.

Brownell, Susan. "Introduction." In Brownell, *The 1904 Anthropology Days and Olympic Games*.

———, ed. *The Anthropology Days and Olympic Games: Sport, Race, and American Imperialism*. Lincoln: University of Nebraska Press, 2008.

Bruner, Frank G. "The Hearing of Primitive Peoples." *Archives of Psychology* 2, no. 11 (1908). New York: The Science Press, 1911.

Buel, J. W., ed. *Louisiana and the Fair*. St. Louis: World's Progress Publishing, 1904.

Bushman, Richard. *Joseph Smith: A Rough Stone Rolling.* New York: Vintage Books, 2007.

Cabajsky, Andrea. "Catholic Gothic: Atavism, Orientalism, and Genetic Change in Charles De Guise's *Le Capau Diable.*" In *Unsettled Remains: Canadian Literature and Postcolonial Gothic,* edited by Cynthia Sugars and Gerry Turcotte, 1–29. Ontario: Wilfrid Laurier University, 2009.

Census of the Philippine Islands. 1903. Washington, DC: US Bureau of the Census, 1905.

Chakrabarty, Dipesh. *Provincializing Euorpe: Postcolonial Thought and Historical Difference* (Princeton: Princeton University Press, 2007).

Clevenger, Martha R., ed. *"Indescribably Grand": Diaries and Letters from the 1904 World's Fair.* St. Louis: Missouri Historical Society Press, 1996.

Clifford, James. "On Ethnographic Allegory." In *Writing Culture: The Poetics and Politics of Ethnography,* edited by James Clifford and George E. Marcus, 98–121. Berkeley: University of California Press, 1986.

Cohn, Bernard S. *Colonialism and Its Forms of Knowledge: The British in India.* Princeton, NJ: Princeton University Press, 1996.

Collingham, Elizabeth M. *Imperial Bodies: The Physical Experience of the Raj, c. 1800–1947.* Cambridge, MA: Polity Press, 2001.

Cooper, Frederick. *Colonialism in Question: Theory, Knowledge, History.* Berkeley: University of California Press, 2005.

Corbey, Raymond. "Ethnographic Showcases, 1870–1930." *Cultural Anthropology* 8, no. 3 (August 1993): 338–69.

Crew, Spencer R., and James E. Sims. "Locating Authenticity: Fragments of a Dialogue." In Karp and Lavine, *Exhibiting Cultures,* 159–175.

Culbertson, Kurt. "George Edward Kessler, Landscape Architect of the American Renaissance." In *Midwestern Landscape Architecture,* edited by W. H. Tishler, 99–116. Urbana: University of Illinois Press, 2000.

Day, Tony. *Fluid Iron: State Formation in Southeast Asia.* Honolulu: University of Hawaii Press, 2002.

Day, Tony, and Craig J. Reynolds. "Cosmologies, Truth Regimes, and the State in Southeast Asia." *Modern Asian Studies* 34, no. 1 (February 2000): 1–55.

Dyreson, Mark. *Making the American Team: Sport, Culture, and the Olympic Experience.* Champaign: University of Illinois Press, 1997.

Edgerton, Ron K. "Americans, Cowboys, and Cattlemen on the Mindanao Frontier." In *Reappraising an Empire: New Perspectives on Philippine-American History,* edited by Peter W. Stanley, 237–59. Cambridge, MA: Harvard University Press, 1984.

English, Leo James. *English-Tagalog Dictionary.* Quezon City: Kalayaan Press, 1977.

"'Extract from Democratic Campaign Book—1902.' Democratic Platform. Adopted at Kansas City, July 4, 1900." In Bureau of Insular Affairs, RG 350, Box 1, Special Records Relating to the Philippine Islands. National Archives, College Park, Maryland.

Fabian, Johannes. *Time and the Other: How Anthropology Makes Its Object.* New York: Columbia University Press, 2002.

Fermin, Jose D. *1904 World's Fair: The Filipino Experience.* Quezon City: University of the Philippines Press, 2004.

50 Years with the Times. Compiled by Raul R. Ingles. National Library of the Philippines, Rare Books and Manuscripts, Filipiniana Section, Manila, Philippines.

The History of Sexuality, Vol. 1: An Introduction. New York: Vintage Books, 1978.

Francis, David R. *The Universal Exposition of 1904.* St. Louis: Louisiana Purchase Exposition Company, 1913.

Fritzsche, Peter. *Stranded in the Present: Modern Time and the Melancholy of History.* Cambridge, MA: Harvard University Press, 2004.

Gilbert, James. "World's Fairs as Historical Events." In Rydell and Gwinn, *Fair Representations,* 21–79.

Gonzalez, Vernadette V. "Headhunter Itineraries: The Philippines as America's Dream Jungle." *Global South* 3, no. 2 (Fall 2009): 144–72.

Gowing, Peter G. *Mandate in Moroland: The American Government of Muslim Filipinos, 1899–1920.* Quezon City: Philippine Center for Advanced Studies, University of the Philippines, 1977.

Gowing, Peter G., and Robert D. McAmis, eds. *The Muslim Filipinos.* Manila: Solidaridad Publishing House, 1974.

Haeri, Shaykh Fadhlalla. *The Elements of Sufism.* New York: Barnes and Noble, 1999.

Hall, G. Stanley. *Adolescence: Its Psychology and Its Relations to Physiology, Anthropology, Sociology, Sex, Crime, Religion, and Education.* Vols. 1–2. New York: D. Appleton, 1904.

Hartley, William G. "Missouri's 1838 Extermination Order and the Mormon's Forced Removal to Illinois." *Mormon Historical Studies* 2, no. 1 (2001): 5–27.

Hawkins, Michael C. "Frontier Justice, Colonial Justice, and the Spaces In Between in the Southern Philippines, 1898–1913." *Siliman Journal* 53, no. 1 (October 2012): 193–206.

———. "Imperial Historicism and American Military Rule in the Philippines' Muslim South." *Journal of Southeast Asian Studies* 39, no. 3 (October 2008): 411–29.

———. *Making Moros: Imperial Historicism and American Military Rule in the Philippines' Muslim South.* DeKalb: Northern Illinois University Press, 2013.

———. "Managing a Massacre: Savagery, Civility and Gender in Moro Province in the Wake of Bud Dajo." *Philippine Studies* 58, no. 1 (2011): 81–103.

———. "Masculinity Reborn: Chivalry, Misogyny, Potency and Violence in the Philippines' Muslim South, 1899–1914." *Journal of Southeast Asian Studies* 44, no. 2 (June 2013): 250–65.

———. "Undecided Empire: The Travails of Imperial Representation of Filipinos at the Greater America Exposition, 1899." *Philippine Studies: Historical and Ethnographic Viewpoints* 63, no. 3 (September 2015): 341–63.

Heinemann, F. H. "Reply to Historicism." *Philosophy* 21, no. 80 (November 1946): 245–57.

Hofstadter, Richard. *The Paranoid Style in American Politics.* New York: Knopf, 1965.

Hoganson, Kristin L. *Fighting for American Manhood: How Gender Politics Provoked the Spanish-American and Philippine-American Wars.* New Haven: Yale University Press, 1998.

Hoit, T. W. *The Right of American Slavery.* St. Louis: L. Bushnell, 1860.

Holt, Thomas C. "Marking: Race, Race-Making, and the Writing of History." *American Historical Review* 100, no. 10 (February 1995): 1–20.

Hunt, James. *The Negro's Place in Nature: A Paper Read Before the London Anthropological Society.* New York: Van Evrie, Horton, 1866.

Hurley, Vic. *Swish of the Kris: The Story of the Moros.* New York: E.P. Dutton, 1936.

Utley, H. T. "The History of Slavery and Emancipation." Speech delivered before the Democratic Association in Dubuque, Iowa, February 12, 1863. Philadelphia: John Campbell Publisher, 1863.

Ibrahim, Ahmad, Sharon Siddique, and Yasmin Hussain, eds. *Readings on Islam in Southeast Asia.* Singapore: Institute of Southeast Asian Studies, 1985.

Ileto, Reynaldo C. *Filipinos and Their Revolution: Event, Discourse, and Historiography.* Manila: Ateneo de Manila University Press, 1998.

———. *Pasyon and Revolution: Popular Movements in the Philippines, 1840–1910.* Manila: Ateneo de Manila University Press, 1979.

Jackson, C. S., et al. *Jackson's Famous Photographs of the Louisiana Purchase Exposition.* Chicago: Metropolitan Syndicate Press, 1904.

Jacobson, Cardell K., and Lara Burton. *Modern Polygamy in the United States: Historical, Cultural and Legal Issues.* New York: Oxford University Press, 2011.

Jones, Mary Ellen, ed. *The American Frontier: Opposing Viewpoints.* San Diego: Greenhaven Press, 1994.

Joseph, Betty. *Reading the East India Company, 1720–1840: Colonial Currencies of Gender.* Chicago: University of Chicago Press, 2004.

Karp, Ivan. "Culture and Representation." In Karp and Lavine, *Exhibiting Cultures,* 11–24.

Karp, Ivan, and Steven D. Lavine, eds. *Exhibiting Cultures: The Poetics and Politics of Museum Display.* Washington, DC: Smithsonian Institution, 1991.

Kirshenblatt-Gimblett, Barbara. "Objects of Ethnography." In Karp and Lavine, *Exhibiting Cultures,* 386–443.

Kramer, Paul A. *The Blood of Government: Race, Empire, the United States, and the Philippines.* Chapel Hill: University of North Carolina Press, 2006.

———. "Making Concessions: Race and Empire Revisited at the Philippine Exposition, St. Louis, 1901–1905." *Radical History Review* 73 (1999): 74–114.

Kurtz, Charles M. *The St. Louis World's Fair of 1904.* St. Louis: Gottschalk Printing Company, 1903.

Laqueur, Thomas. *Making Sex: Body and Gender from the Greeks to Freud.* Cambridge, MA: Harvard University Press, 1992.

Lavine, Steven D. "Art Museums, National Identity, and the Status of Minority Cultures: The Case of Hispanic Art in the United States." In Karp and Lavine, *Exhibiting Cultures,* 79–87.

Lears, T. J. Jackson. "From Salvation to Self-Realization: Advertising and the Therapeutic Roots of the Consumer Culture, 1880–1930." In *The Culture of Consumption: Critical Essays in American History, 1880–1980,* edited by Richard Wightman Fox and T. J. Jackson Lears, 1–38. New York: Pantheon Books, 1983.

———. *No Place of Grace: Antimodernism and the Transformation of American Culture, 1880–1920.* Chicago: University of Chicago Press, 1981.

Lee, Dwight E., and Robert N. Beck. "The Meaning of 'Historicism.'" *American Historical Review* 59, no. 3 (April 1954): 568–77.

Lewisohn, Leonard, ed. *The Heritage of Sufism*. Boston: Oneworld, 1999.

Liebel, Helen P. "The Enlightenment and the Rise of Historicism in German Thought." *Eighteenth-Century Studies* 4, no. 4 (Summer 1971): 359–85.

Lopez, Sixto. *"Tribes" in the Philippines*. Boston: New England Anti-Imperialist League, 1900.

Louisiana purchase exposition board. *Official Handbook of the Philippines and Catalogue of the Philippine Exhibit*. 2 vols. Ann Arbor, Michigan: University of Michigan Library, 2005. First published 1903 by Bureau of Public Printing (Manila).

Lowenstein, M. J., comp. *Official Guide, Louisiana Purchase Exposition—Souvenir Edition*. St. Louis: The Official Guide Company, 1904.

Lyons, Paul. *American Pacifism: American Explorations of the Colonialism, Race, Gender and Sexuality*. New York: Routledge, 2005.

MacLaury, Robert E. "Linguistic Relativity and the Plasticity of Categorization: Universalism in a New Key." In *Explorations in Linguistic Relativity*, edited by Martin Putz and Jarjolijn H. Verspoor, 249–94. Amsterdam: John Benjamins, 2000.

Majul, Cesar A. *The Historical Background of the Muslims in the Philippines and the Present Mindanao Crisis*. Marawi City: Printed under the auspices of the Ansar El Islam as a background material on the occasion of its second National Islamic Symposium and third foundation anniversary, 1972.

———. *Muslims in the Philippines*. Quezon City: University of the Philippines Press, 1973.

Mangan, J. A., and James Walvin, eds. *Manliness and Morality: Middle-Class Masculinity in Britain and America, 1800–1940*. Manchester: Manchester University Press, 1987.

Marr, Timothy. *The Cultural Roots of American Islamicism*. Cambridge: Cambridge University Press, 2006.

Marx, Karl, and Frederick Engels. *The Communist Manifesto*. New York: International Publishers, 2014.

Massaquoi, Hans J. "Lefties—A Maligned Minority." *Ebony* 22, no. 7 (May 1967): 63–69.

Mastura, Michael O. "Muslim Scholars and Social Science Research: Some Notes on Muslim Studies in the Philippines." In *Muslim Social Science in ASEAN*, edited by Omar Farouk Bajunid, 23–46. Kuala Lumpur: Yayasan Penataran Ilmu, 1994.

McCarthy, Cormac. *Blood Meridian: Or the Evening Redness in the West*. New York: Vintage, 1992.

McGee, William J. "Anthropology." *World's Fair Bulletin* 5, no. 4 (February 1904): 4–9.

———. "Anthropology at the Louisiana Purchase Exposition." *Science*, n.s., vol. 22, no. 573 (December 22, 1905): 815–23.

———. "The Trend of Human Progress." *American Anthropologist*, n.s., vol. 1, no. 3 (July 1899): 401–47.

McKinley, William. "Benevolent Assimilation Proclamation," December 21, 1898. In *Documentary Sources of Philippine History*, compiled, edited, and annotated by Gregorio F. Zaide, 287–88. Manila: National Book Store, 1990.

Mendoza, Victor Roman. *Metroimperial Intimacies: Fantasy, Racial-Sexual Governance, and the Philippines in U.S. Imperialism, 1899–1913.* Durham: Duke University Press, 2015.

Mondale, Sarah, ed. *School: The Story of American Public Education.* New York: Beacon Press, 2002.

Morgan, Lewis H. *Ancient Society or Researches in the Lines of Human Progress from Savagery Through Barbarism to Civilization.* London: MacMillan, 1877.

Moss, Robert. "The 1904 World's Fair: A Turning Point for American Food." *Serious Eats,* January 11, 2016. http://www.seriouseats.com/2016/01/food-history-1904-worlds-fair-st-louis.html.

Mrozek, Donald J. "The Habit of Victory: The American Military and the Cult of Manliness." In Mangan and Walvin, *Manliness and Morality,* 220–41.

Mutalib, Hussin. *Islam in Southeast Asia.* Singapore: Institute of Southeast Asian Studies, 2008.

Nathan, K. S., and Mohammad Hashim Kamali. *Islam in Southeast Asia: Political, Social and Strategic Challenges for the 21st Century.* Singapore: Institute of Southeast Asian Studies, 2005.

The Official Souvenir Program of the Philippines Carnival, February 27–March 3, 1908. American Historical Collection, Rizal Library, Ateneo de Manila University, Philippines.

Parezo, Nancy J. "A 'Special Olympics.'" In *The 1904 Anthropology Days and Olympic Games: Sport, Race, and American Imperialism,* edited by Susan Brownell, 59–126. Lincoln: University of Nebraska Press, 2008.

Parezo, Nancy J., and Don D. Fowler. *Anthropology Goes to the Fair: The 1904 Louisiana Purchase Exposition.* Lincoln: University of Nebraska Press, 2007.

Patnaik, Prabhat. "Historicism and Revolution." *Social Scientist* 32, no. 1–2 (January–February 2004): 30–41.

Peterson, William. *Places for Happiness: Community, Self, and Performance in the Philippines.* Honolulu: University of Hawaii Press, 2016.

Philippine Carnival. Official Handbook, Manila, February 2–9, 1909. American Historical Collection, Rizal Library, Ateneo de Manila University, Philippines.

Philippines: Handbook and Catalogue of the Philippine Exhibit, St. Louis, 1904. From Records of the Bureau of Insular Affairs, Special Records Relating to the Philippine Islands, Miscellaneous Records, ca. 1893–1932, RG 350, Box 2, US National Archives, College Park, Maryland.

Pink, Sarah, Laszlo Kurti, and Ana Isabel Alfonso. *Working Images: Visual Research and Representation in Ethnography.* New York: Routledge, 2004.

Polynesian Cultural Center home page. https://www.polynesia.com/villages/#.WoHJ9ZM-d-U.

"Polynesian Cultural Center to Launch Million Visitor per Year Strategic Initiative." *Business Wire* 27 (April 2017). https://businesswire.com/news/home/20170427006333/en/Polynesian-Cultural-Center-Launch-Million-Visitor-Year.

Pratt, Mary Louise. *Imperial Eyes: Travel Writing and Transculturation.* 2nd ed. New York: Routledge, 2007.

Quizon, Cherubim A., and Patricia O. Afable. "Rethinking Displays of Filipinos at St. Louis: Embracing Heartbreak and Irony." *Philippine Studies* 52, no. 4 (2004): 439–44.

Rafael, Vicente. *Contracting Colonialism: Translation and Christian Conversion in Tagalog Society under Early Spanish Rule*. Ithaca: Cornell University Press, 1988.

———. *Nationalism and the Technics of Translation in the Spanish Philippines*. Durham: Duke University Press, 2005.

———. *White Love and Other Events in Filipino History*. Durham: Duke University Press, 2000.

Reid, Anthony. *Slavery, Bondage, and Dependency in Southeast Asia*. New York: St. Martin's Press, 1983.

Report of the Philippine Exposition Board to the Louisiana Purchase Exposition. St. Louis: Greeley Printery of St. Louis, 1904.

Report of the Philippine Exposition Board. Washington, DC: Bureau of Insular Affairs, War Department, 1905.

Reports of the Philippine Commission. Washington, DC: Government Printing Office, 1900–1913.

Republican Party Platform of 1856. June 18, 1856.

Reynolds, Craig J. "A New Look at Old Southeast Asia." *Journal of Asian Studies* 54, no. 2 (May 1995): 419–46.

Roberts, B. H. *Comprehensive History of the Church of Jesus Christ of Latter-Day Saints*. Vol. 1. Salt Lake City: Deseret News Press, 1930.

Rodil, B. R. *The Story of Mindanao and Sulu in Question and Answer*. Davao: MINCODE, 2003.

Roosevelt, Theodore. *Winning of the West*. Vols. 1–4. Presidential ed. Lincoln: University of Nebraska Press, 1995.

Rosaldo, Renato. "Imperialist Nostalgia." *Representations* 26, special issue: Memory and Counter-Memory (Spring 1989): 107–22.

Rossi, Pietro. "The Ideological Valences of Twentieth-Century Historicism." *History and Theory* 14, no. 4, Beiheft 14: Essays on Historicism (December 1975): 15–29.

Rydell, Robert W. *All the World's a Fair: Visions of Empire at American International Expositions, 1876–1916*. Chicago: University of Chicago Press, 1984.

Rydell, Robert W., and Nancy Gwinn, eds. *Fair Representations: World's Fairs and the Modern World*. Amsterdam: VU University Press, 1994.

Said, Edward W. *Culture and Imperialism*. New York: Vintage Books, 1993.

———. *Orientalism*. New York: Vintage Books, 1979.

Salman, Michael. *The Embarrassment of Slavery: Controversies over Bondage and Nationalism in the American Colonial Philippines*. Berkeley: University of California Press, 2001.

Samuel, Lawrence L. *The End of Innocence: The 1964–1965 New York World's Fair*. Syracuse: Syracuse University Press, 2007.

Schrecker, John. *The Chinese Revolution in Historical Perspective*. Westport: Praeger, 2004.

Scott, Hugh L. *Some Memories of a Soldier*. New York: Century Company, 1928.

Scott, James C. *The Moral Economy of the Peasant: Rebellion and Subsistence in Southeast Asia*. New Haven: Yale University Press, 1976.

———. "Patron-Client Politics and Political Change in Southeast Asia." In *Friends, Followers, and Factions: A Reader in Political Clientism*, edited by S. W. Schmidt et al., 123–46. Berkeley: University of California Press, 1977.

Shipman, Pat. *The Evolution of Racism*. Cambridge, MA: Harvard University Press, 1994.

Sinclair, Upton. *The Jungle*. New York: Dover, 2001.

Slotkin, Richard. *The Fatal Environment: The Myth of the Frontier in the Age of Industrialization, 1800–1890*. Norman: University of Oklahoma Press, 1998.

———. *Gunfighter Nation: The Myth of the Frontier in Twentieth Century America*. Norman: University of Oklahoma Press, 1998.

———. *Regeneration through Violence: The Mythology of the American Frontier, 1600–1860*. Norman: University of Oklahoma Press, 2000.

Souvenir of the Philippine Exposition. Manila Review of Trade and Price Current, 1904.

Souvenir Visayan Village. St. Louis: Philippine Photograph Company, 1904.

Starr, Chester G. "Historical and Philosophical Time." *History and Theory* 6, Beiheft 6: History and the Concept of Time (1966): 24–35.

Stoler, Ann Laura. *Carnal Knowledge and Imperial Power: Race and the Intimate in Colonial Rule*. Berkeley: University of California Press, 2002.

———. "Rethinking Colonial Categories: European Communities and the Boundaries of Rule." *Comparative Studies in Society and History* 31, no. 1 (January 1989): 134–61.

Stoler, Ann Laura, and Frederick Cooper. "Between Metropole and Colony: Rethinking a Research Agenda." In *Tensions of Empire: Colonial Cultures in a Bourgeois World*, edited by Frederick Cooper and Ann Laura Stoler, 1–58. Berkeley: University of California Press, 1997.

Stringfellow, Thornton. *A Brief Examination of Scripture Testimony on the Institution of Slavery*. Washington, DC: Congressional Globe Office, 1850.

Sullivan, James E. *Spalding's Official Athletic Almanac for 1905*. New York: American Publishing Company, 1905.

Sweet, Owen. "The Moro, the Fighting-Man of the Philippines." *Harper's Weekly*, June 9, 1906.

Tan, Samuel K. *Sulu under American Military Rule, 1899–1913*. Quezon City: University of the Philippines Press, 1968.

Tasker Bliss Papers. Microfilm and microfiche sections, National Library of the Philippines, Manila.

Thomas, Nicholas. *Colonialism's Culture: Anthropology, Travel and Government*. Princeton, NJ: Princeton University Press, 1994.

Thompson, C. Blancher. *The Nachash Origin of the Black and Mixed Races*. St. Louis: George Knapp & Co., Printers and Binders, 1860.

Thomson, James C. Jr., Peter W. Stanley, and John C. Perry. *Sentimental Imperialists: The American Experience in East Asia*. New York: Harper and Row, 1981.

Tompkins, E. Berkeley. *Anti-imperialism in the United States: The Great Debate, 1890–1920*. Philadelphia: University of Pennsylvania Press, 1970.

Trimingham, J. Spencer. *The Sufi Orders in Islam*. London: Oxford University Press, 1998.

Turner, Frederick Turner. "The Significance of the Frontier in American History." In Annual Report of the American Historical Association for the Year 1893. US Congressional Serial Set, No. 3170.

———. *The Frontier in American History.* Henry Holt, 1920.

Vandiver, Frank E. *Black Jack: The Life and Times of John J. Pershing.* College Station: Texas A&M University Press, 1977.

Vergara, Benito M. Jr. *Displaying Filipinos: Photography and Colonialism in Early 20th Century Philippines.* Quezon City: University of the Philippines Press, 1995.

Walker, John B. "What the Louisiana Purchase Exposition Is." *Cosmopolitan* 38, no. 5 (September 1904): 599–603.

War Department Annual Reports, 1908. Vol. 7, pt. 1. Washington, DC: Government Printing Office, 1909.

Warren, James. *The Global Economy and the Sulu Zone: Connections, Commodities, and Culture.* Quezon City: New Day, 2000.

———. "The Iranun and Balangingi Slaving Voyage: Middle Passages in the Sulu Zone." In *Many Middle Passages*, edited by Christopher, Emma, Pybus, Cassandra, Rediker, Marcus, 52–71. Berkeley: University of California Press, 2007.

———. "The Port of Jolo: International Trade and Slave Raiding." In *Pirates, Ports, and Coasts in Asia: Historical and Contemporary Perspectives*, edited by Kleinen, John and Osseweijer, Manon, 178–99. Singapore: Institute of Southeast Asian Studies, 2007.

———. "Ransom, Escape and Debt Repayment in the Sulu Zone, 1750–1898." In *Bonded Labour and Debt in the Indian Ocean World*, edited by Stanziani, Alessandro and Campbell, Gwyn, 87–101. London: Pickering and Chatto, 2013.

———. "Saltwater Slavers and Captives in the Sulu Zone, 1768–1878." *Slavery and Abolition: A Journal of Slave and Post-slave Studies* 31, no. 3 (2010): 429–49.

———. "Slave Markets and Exchange in the Malay World: The Sulu Sultanate, 1770–1878." *Journal of Southeast Asian Studies* 8, no. 2 (1977): 162–75.

———. "The Structure of Slavery in the Sulu Zone in the Late Eighteenth and Nineteenth Centuries." *Slavery and Abolition: A Journal of Slave and Post-slave Studies* 24 (2010): 111–28.

———. *The Sulu Zone, 1768–1898: The Dynamics of External Trade, Slavery and Ethnicity in the Transformation of a Southeast Asian Maritime State.* Singapore: Singapore University Press, 1981.

———. *The Sulu Zone: The World Capitalist Economy and the Historical Imagination.* Amsterdam: VU University Press, 1998.

Warren, R. W. *Nellie Norton: or Southern Slavery and the Bible.* Macon: Burke, Boykin and Company, 1864.

Worcester, Dean. *The Philippines Past and Present.* New York: Macmillan Press, 1914.

White, John Roberts. *Bullets and Bolos: Fifteen Years in the Philippine Islands.* New York: Century, 1928.

Yengoyan, Aram A. "Culture, Ideology and World's Fairs: Colonizer and Colonized in Comparative Perspectives." In Rydell and Gwinn, *Fair Representations*.

Young, Robert J. C. *Colonial Desire: Hybridity in Theory, Culture, and Race.* New York: Routledge, 1995.

Zachman, Jon B. "The Legacy and Meaning of World's Fair Souvenirs." In Rydell and Gwinn, *Fair Representations*, 203–37.

INDEX

CPSIA information can be obtained
at www.ICGtesting.com
Printed in the USA
BVHW031957310120
571130BV00002B/15/J

9 781501 748219